Mountains So Sublime

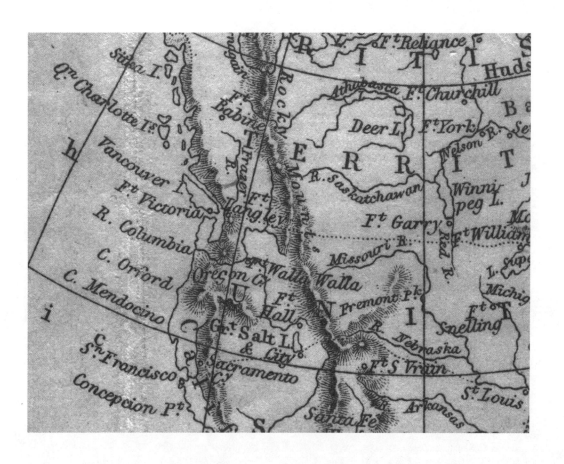

Mountains So Sublime

NINETEENTH-CENTURY BRITISH TRAVELLERS AND
THE LURE OF THE ROCKY MOUNTAIN WEST

Terry Abraham

COVER.   Panoramic view of the Rocky Mountains from Kishenston stations. North American Boundary Commission Photographs. No. 66–68, 1861. Courtesy Royal Engineers Corps Library Chatham, Kent, England.

FRONTISPIECE. MAP OF THE NORTH AMERICAN WEST. Map of North America. Richard Francis Burton. *The City of the Saints, and Across the Rocky Mountains to California.* New York, Harper & Brothers, 1862. opp. p. 1 (detail). Courtesy University of Idaho Library.

Published by the University of Calgary Press
2500 University Drive NW
Calgary, Alberta, Canada T2N 1N4
www.uofcpress.com

We acknowledge the financial support of the Government of Canada, through the Book Publishing Industry Development Program (BPIDP), and the Alberta Foundation for the Arts for our publishing activities. We acknowledge the support of the Canada Council for the Arts for our publishing program.

Library and Archives Canada Cataloguing in Publication

Abraham, Terry P
Mountains so sublime : nineteenth-century British travellers and the lure of the Rocky Mountain West / Terry Abraham.
Includes bibliographical references and index.

ISBN 10: 1-55238-181-1 (University of Calgary Press)
ISBN 13: 978-1-55238-181-6 (University of Calgary Press)

ISBN 10: 0-87013-791-3 (Michigan State University Press)
ISBN 13: 978-1-87013-791-4 (Michigan State University Press)

1. British – Rocky Mountains – History – 19th century – Sources. 2. Travelers – Rocky Mountains – History – 19th century – Sources. 3. Rocky Mountains – Description and travel. 4. Rocky Mountains – History – 19th century – Sources. 5. Travelers' writings, British. I. Title.
FC219.A27 2006   917.804'2'092241   C2006-901082-X

Cover design,
Mieka West

Internal design & typesetting,
Garet Markvoort, zijn digital.

  This book is printed on acid-free paper.

Printed and bound in Canada by Houghton Boston.

Table of Contents

List of Illustrations

Preface

This compilation and discussion of British travellers' eyewitness accounts of their experiences in the North American West had its genesis in a convergence of opportunities. During some three decades as a special collections librarian in the centre of the vast Inland Northwest, that area between the Columbia River and the Bitterroot Mountains, I developed a close acquaintanceship with the texts that document the history and development of the West. Knowledge of the books, however, did not extend to more than a brief introduction to their contents. In 1993, through the support of the University of Idaho Sabbatical Leave Committee, the University of Idaho Research Council, and the Idaho Library Association (as well as a later research fellowship from the Idaho Humanities Council), I had an opportunity to actually read these primary sources both in this country and in libraries in England. My reading served, surprisingly, to reintroduce me to the natural landscape of the

West. Seeing it through the eyes of nineteenth-century British travellers renewed in me a sense of appreciation for my native land.

I was born in the morning shadow of looming Mt. Hood, a magnificent volcanic peak in the Cascades of Oregon. Mt. Hood, like its companion towering over Seattle, was named by George Vancouver after a British admiral. Although mostly an armchair traveller, like the original readers of these accounts, my own travels throughout the West have been widespread and my mode of transportation has been varied. I cannot claim to have suffered the hardships of those early British travellers whose adventures make modern travel seem simple and efficient by comparison. However, I have travelled on foot and by automobile, bus, motorcycle, train, plane, and raft over great parts of the West.

I have hiked along portions of the famed Lewis and Clark Trail near Lolo Pass. My automobile trips have been the most numerous, ranging from superhighways to primitive dirt roads in Idaho's precipitous central mountains. The territory encompasses much of what Paul Fountain called, in 1906, "The Eleven Eaglets of the West:" Arizona, California, Colorado, Idaho, Montana, Nevada, New Mexico, Oregon, Utah, Washington, and Wyoming.[1] The bus has taken me into the mountains above Denver to explore Cripple Creek and Central City in Colorado. I have travelled by motorcycle across Washington State and British Columbia, and down Idaho's panhandle and through the great Snake River Plain. By train, as difficult as it is these days, I have followed some of the same tracks as many of the early travellers on the transcontinental routes; from Omaha through Denver to Salt Lake, from Chicago to Seattle, from Vancouver to Banff, and down the central coastal valleys to Oakland, California. My airplane travel has ranged from massive jets on transpolar routes to small propeller-driven commuter planes skimming over magnificent mountains and rugged canyon lands. In addition, I have enjoyed rafting down portions of Idaho's Snake, Salmon, and Clearwater Rivers.

While I have not yet been to each and every place described by the British travellers in the following accounts, I have been to many of them and so can compare what they described with what I have seen. Recognizing that their descriptions did not always match today's reality was one of the driving forces behind this project. Another impetus was the growing realization that, in writing of their experiences, these travellers were trying to share something of their perceptions and appreciation for this landscape. Today's readers, I believe, can find much of interest and some enlightenment in seeing the West through these earlier eyes.

The West is a big place and I would suggest that my West may not be the same as your West. To other Pacific Northwesterners, for instance, Denver is "back East." Because of my own heritage, North America's Far West, sweeping from the Rockies to the Pacific, is of most importance to me. I was born here and have lived here for almost all of my adult life. It is my home and, until I began reading these accounts, it was very familiar to me. My pleasure in reading these descriptions arises from the shock of unfamiliarity coupled with the frequent recognition of

places and things. It is both different and similar to the present day.

A modern British traveller, former Londoner Jonathan Raban writing in *Passage to Juneau*,[2] argued that time has devalued those earlier observations: "Two centuries of romanticism, much of it routine and degenerate, has blunted everyone's ability to look at waterfalls and precipices in other than dusty and second-hand terms." Following Vancouver's route through British Columbia's inland passage, he "sailed through a logjam of dead literary cliché: snow-capped peaks above, fathomless depths below, and, in the middle of the picture, the usual gaunt cliffs, hoary crags, wild woods, and crystal cascades." My reading in the landscape was the opposite; I found the earlier descriptions so vivid and so characteristic of their time that they provided a new way of seeing the West.

The geographical boundaries of this project were as broad and as vast as the West itself. On the East, the prairie views of the Front Range were one arbitrary boundary. On the West, the Pacific Ocean provided a natural one for this study. The Colorado River to the south and Canada's Peace River to the north provided another set. The inclusion of the Canadian West follows naturally from my own Canadian heritage.[3] The project was bounded in time as well. The discovery of gold in California in 1848, with its influx of emigrants and travellers from all parts of the world, provided one limit. At the other end, the American introduction to British-style imperialism during the Spanish-American War provided the other boundary, with some exceptions.[4] The latter half of the nineteenth century was an era of great change in American and Canadian life, and the West was where many of these changes took place.

These highly arbitrary boundaries in space and time are not absolutes. There have been occasions where an example or illustration may have been drawn from beyond these limits. This is in part because the development of any particular area in the West had its own timeline and sequence of events, making generalizations about chronology and sequence very difficult. In particular, it

has been pointed out to me that the one or two references to giant redwood trees might suggest to some that they are common among the Rocky Mountains instead of isolated in northern California's coast range.

Similarly, the main tenor of the project was to concentrate on British travellers, although some Irish, Scots, and Welsh have also contributed their views. The historian Oscar Winther thought it important to "be very careful to make distinctions between the English, Scots, and Welsh."[5] It seemed inappropriate and ineffective to apply an ethnic test to the authors I have read. The difficulty in doing so has been identified by the humorist George Mikes: "When people say England, they sometimes mean Great Britain, sometimes the United Kingdom, sometimes the British Isles – but never England."[6] My own background as an American of English, Irish, Welsh, Canadian, and German-Russian heritage may have influenced this decision.

Winther reinforced his distinctions by telling the stereotypical story "of a couple of each [group] who were placed, experimentally, on an island, each pair separated from the others. When contacted six months later, the Scots were manufacturing Scotch whiskey, the Welsh were singing hymns lustily together, but the two Englishmen had remained all this while separated from each other – they had not been introduced."[7] I seldom experienced the purported standoffishness exemplified by the latter stereotype during my trips to England, nor in my interaction with Britons visiting the United States.

There is an extensive literature on British travellers in North America, yet most earlier studies have, as their purpose, sought to exalt the Yankee original – the American yeoman whose democratic ways (demonstrated in what appeared to be uncivilized rudeness to the class-bound Brits) proved the superiority of the United States' constitutional experiment. There is, accordingly, no similar literature in Canada. Such concentration on the travellers' observations of political and social affairs excludes a significant component of the travellers' tales: their reports on the North American landscape. Elk hunters, as an example, are usually discounted as observers because they devoted more words to the chase and to the landscape than they did to the people living on that landscape. Here, I attempt to give these sharp-eyed observers their overdue recognition. Accordingly, my choice of sources attempts to recover these tales, and is not comprehensive.

The first chapter serves as an introduction to many of the key players and the landscape they described. It focuses on the travellers' first impression of the monumental Rocky Mountains, whether from the east or the west. The second chapter delves more deeply into the biographies and travelling experiences of the eyewitnesses. Their personal histories contributed to their travel experiences and shaped their narratives of westward travel. Chapter three concentrates on five "literary" types: three major authors, a poet, and a journalist/explorer. Their contributions to the genre are examined and located within the scope of their lives. The next chapter is primarily a discussion of nineteenth-century ways of looking at landscape, describing a cultural background common to our many western travellers. What they looked at, what they saw, and what they reported is evaluated in terms of the societal norms. Chapter five returns to the landscape, where descriptive passages written about specific landforms are presented and compared. The sixth chapter is also comparative; it presents the British travellers' observations of the particular attitudes toward landscape held by the local inhabitants. The final chapter, "Lost Landscapes," answers the question, "What message do these nineteenth-century wanderers have for today's inhabitants of the western landscape?"

These travellers' texts demonstrate the prominence of the landscape surrounding their often querulous comments on the American people. Above all else, it was the Rocky Mountains themselves – and their plateaus and tributary streams – that sent scientists, explorers, tourists, missionaries, and merchants into their lexical caches, seeking out the right words to convey to a British audience the immensity of their subject (which also represented themselves as an obstacle to so many of their plans). In documenting their observations, the travellers added to the growing realization that North American scenery was a unique contribution to the world's natural and cultural heritage. Although their descriptions of the landscape of the North American West have been largely overshadowed by their perceptive observations on the denizens of that place, it was the landscape that ultimately shaped the westerner.[8] This is evident in today's controversies over livestock grazing, mineral rights, fish runs, timber cutting, and waste site placement.

Published and manuscript travellers' accounts of the Rocky Mountain West – some thirty of which are reviewed here – both contributed to and conflicted with North Americans' changing views of their landscape. Although British travellers made few direct comparisons to British landscapes, they often fitted their views to European scenes. Over the fifty years that saw so many changes in the American West, the British were among those who sounded the note of caution. Oscar Wilde, after praising the Rockies and

Ohio's Miami River to a Dayton, Ohio group, cautioned, "You should never let your manufacturers pollute the air with smoke."[9]

This sense of environmental consciousness, as a recognition of the force of people upon the landscape, gives the purely descriptive passages – wonderful as they are – an even stronger emotive power. British travellers were conscious of the many changes taking place around them, and they observed that the inviolate mountains were being blemished and desecrated. While seldom directly referenced, these writers were surely aware of the effect of human activities on their own landscape back home. Like the English countryside, the West was neither too vast nor too big to escape being overused and overmanaged. Today's readers, I believe, can find much of interest and some enlightenment in seeing the West through these earlier eyes.

And finally, I ask only that you join with me in both enjoying and learning from these narratives. Let me repeat the request of British traveller Frank Marryat:

Reader, these pages are so much black and white, and will pass as nearly all such matter does, rapidly to oblivion; but if they bring no smile to you, nor help momentarily to efface a care, I would ask that they should bring no frown, for they are written earnestly, and with a good intention, even though from first to last they stand against me as printed errors, to cause regret in later years.[10]

Acknowledgments

I particularly wish to recognize those who assisted me in the course of this project: Peter Siems, Moscow, Idaho; Susan Armitage, Pullman, Washington; Jennifer O'Laughlin, Interlibrary Loan, University of Idaho Library, Moscow, Idaho; Karyl Winn, Seattle, Washington; Ron Force, Moscow, Idaho; Lynn Baird, Moscow, Idaho; Robert A. Burchell and Jean Campbell, Eccles Centre, British Library, London; David Whittaker, Provo, Utah; Trevor Rowley and Ann Reese, Rewley House, Oxford; Richard Ovenden, National Library of Scotland; Shonnie Finnegan, Buffalo, New York; Molly Solazzo, Rochester, New York; Callie McGinnis, Columbus, Georgia; Holly Hall, St. Louis, Missouri; Mary Beth Christansen, Los Angeles, California; Robin Smith, Edinburgh; Gary Menges, Seattle, Washington; Angela Haggard, San Antonio, Texas; Margaret Redding, Ottawa, Canada; Jack Kessler, San Francisco, California; Brian Rogers, New London, Connecticut; the late Merle Wells, Boise, Idaho; Guila Ford, Boise, Idaho;

the late Peter Palmquist, Arcata, California; Carlos Schwantes, formerly of Moscow, Idaho and now at St. Louis, Missouri; Kathy Barnard, Moscow, Idaho; Tom Trusky, Boise, Idaho; Lori Keenan, formerly of Moscow, Idaho and now in Vancouver, B.C.; Sybil Barnes, Estes Park, Colorado; Eric Paddock, Denver, Colorado; Taylor Pittman, Maggie Magnuson, and Captain Robert T. Arnold, Royal Engineers Corps Library, Chatham, Kent; the late Peggy Pace, Moscow, Idaho; Eric Isaacson, Moscow, Idaho; and Ron Force and MaryJane Bailey of the University of Idaho Library. I am also grateful to many others in several countries who also assisted me.

Appreciation is also extended to the Department of Western Manuscripts, Bodleian Library, Oxford, for permission to quote from the following manuscripts:

Bodley, John E. C.
Diary, 1888. MSS.*Eng.misc.e.461*
Correspondence, 1884–1923. MS.*Eng.lett.e.72*

Hubback, Catherine.
Letters, Oakland, CA, *1871–1876. Ms.Eng.lett.e.150*

Thomson, James.
Diary, May 18–Dec 12, 1872. Ms.Don.e.46
Notebook, 1872. MS.*Don.e.47*

Appreciation is also extended to Hugh A. Hanley, County Archivist, Buckinghamshire Record Office, for permission to quote from the following:

Desborough, William Henry Grenfell, 1st Baron (1855–1945)
Diary, 1884, America and Canada, Mss.D 86/2

Appreciation is also extended to the British Library Reproduction Department for permission to reproduce three illustrations from W. G. Marshall, *Through America; or, Nine Months in the United States* (1881) #1041083.

In addition, appreciation is also extended to the Royal Engineers Corps Library for permission to reproduce six photographs from the North American Boundary Commission Photographs (1861).

The University of Idaho Library has allowed me to make reproductions of the other illustrations in the text, for which I am grateful.

Additionally, I wish to acknowledge the University of Idaho Sabbatical Leave Committee which granted me time to research and write, and to the current and former members of the staff of the Department of Special Collections and Archives at the University of Idaho Library, Richard C. Davis, Christine Gray, Anar Imin, the late Judy Nielsen, and Marilyn Sandmeyer, who made it possible for me to take the time, then and now. Portions of the research were funded by the University of Idaho Research Council, the Idaho Library Association, and the Idaho Humanities Council, a state-based program of the National Endowment for the Humanities. The conclusions or opinions in this work do not necessarily represent the views of any of those organizations.

And the greatest of appreciation is offered to Priscilla Wegars, for everything.

I

First View of the Rockies

Passing Syracuse, we saw a large post labelled "Kansas." In a moment the other side became visible, bearing the name Colorado. "What about the Switzerland of America? This is a horrible desert," we exclaim. "Wait and see," said a fellow traveller; "do you notice that little blue cloud westward? That lies on Pike's Peak. Get there to-morrow, and then talk of Switzerland as you will."[1]

Mountains as Metaphor

Mountains, particularly a range of mountains, evoke awe, wonder, grandeur, and appreciation among today's tourists. As dominant features in the landscape of western North America, the great Rocky Mountains appear in brochures, magazine covers, and advertisements. Yet, to the explorer, surveyor, or emigrant of the mid-nineteenth century, mountains served alternately as mileposts and obstacles. The urge to "go look at the mountains" was the product of a shifting sensibility barely a hundred years old, and it was not usually shared by the struggling pioneer. Just after the mid-nineteenth century, mountains benefited from the concurrence of improved transportation and a well-developed aesthetic appreciation; these areas began to be viewed as destinations instead of obstacles. In seeking the "Switzerland of America," the Alp-like mountains beyond eastern Colorado's western horizon, English journalist Samuel Nugent Townshend was fulfilling the western traveller's objective of going to see the Rockies.

Once among the Rockies, by whatever route or conveyance, the traveller was exposed to a vast and sometimes strange landscape where the natural features overwhelmed the material artifacts of the miner or settler. As a consequence, the Rocky Mountains serve here as a metaphor for the whole of the mountainous west, that region running from the borders of the western plains to the Pacific Ocean, and from the Peace River to the Colorado River. The Continental Divide becomes another metaphor as well, standing in for the mid-nineteenth century's cultural and technological divide, marked as well by the Civil War and the transcontinental railroad.

The latter half of the nineteenth century was a period of immense change, ranging from the discovery of gold in California in 1848 to the United States' defeat of a European navy in Asian waters in 1898. In the West, these changes included the growth of the railroads, the opening of arid lands to settlers, the ongoing quest for mineral wealth, and the increase in urbanization. By 1910, for example, most parts of the West had received their greatest influx of population;

except for the larger urban areas, the population has continued to decline through to the present day.

Pre-eminent among the many eyewitnesses to these changes were the travellers from England; many of them wrote of their experiences in the Rocky Mountain West. British travellers brought to their accounts a different subjectivity than that provided by other travellers. The local inhabitants held a particularly jaundiced view of their surroundings. In fact, those who survived the rigours of the landscape as pioneers were seldom interested in just going to look at it.[2] Rudyard Kipling noted that, "Americans don't mix with their scenery as yet."[3] Easterners, coming from the hills they called mountains, seemed uneasy with the extremes and contrasts of the western landscape.

The English tourist, on the other hand, showed more interest in the power of the scenery, experiencing it directly and gladly. As was said about one Englishwoman: "She was challenged, not cowed, by the majesty and grandeur of the mountains."[4] The Britons were quicker than the Americans in accepting the western landscape as a "Wonderland;" one even proclaimed: "Nothing can be so idyllic as the lesser hills of Colorado, as they stand hemmed in by the weather-beaten peaks which loom up above them in silent majesty. In these America is unrivaled."[5] In addition, the publications of British travellers are important documents of on-site reportage because, as one historian noted, "by and large, these people were literate, intelligent, well-traveled, and above all, not favorably influenced by the local manifest destiny virus."[6]

British travellers of the day contributed to and continued an extensive tradition of travel narratives, all of which provide a large pool of documentation for us today. Back then, there was a considerable audience for these accounts, both in England and North America. The armchair travellers were interested in nearly everything about the West, including the landforms and scenery. In addition, because of the strained relationship between the Britons and their former colonists, there was a great deal of interest in the developing republic's politics and cultural life. That the

Camp in Horse-shoe Park. Arthur Pendarves Vivian.
Wanderings in the Western Land. (1879). p. 145. Courtesy
University of Idaho Library.

northern half of the continent remained British,
albeit with its own distinctive character and history, provided a counterpoint of contrast and
comparison to the United States.

That first, sometimes overwhelming, view of
the Rockies serves as an introduction to British
travellers' accounts of the Rocky Mountain
West. In both published and unpublished
accounts, travellers and tourists described the
Rockies as "glorious," "grand," "great," "magnificent," and "stupendous." The wildness and ruggedness of the mountain ranges were frequently
invoked, often in contrast to park-like meadows
or the emptiness of the plains. Surprisingly, these
are part of a package of sophisticated conventions that were in common use among a literate

and well-travelled populace. A century earlier,
literary sentiment had transformed the concept
of mountains from monstrous entities to sources
of artistic inspiration.[7] Once viewed as majestic and wondrous, mountains began to attract
tourists and travellers. The French, Swiss, and
Italian Alps received the first brunt of this essentially English movement.[8] With the completion
of the transcontinental railroad in 1869, North
America's western mountains opened to the traveller and tourist – if they made the effort to get
off the track.[9] Still, the limitations of the track
were recognized; even Kipling asked: "How
in the world was it possible to take even one-
thousandth of this huge, roaring, many sided
continent?"[10]

Of course, those laying out the tracks got the
best views, but hardly under tourist conditions.
One of the most extreme travel expeditions to
and across the Rocky Mountains was taken by
William Francis Butler of the British Army. He
crossed the Canadian prairie and mountains in
the mid-winter of 1872. In effusive prose, he captured the significance of sighting the Rockies as

a milepost along his journey, comparing them to
the desolate winter landscape of the Prairies:

*It is a remote spot, in a land which is itself remote. From
out of the plain to the west, forty or fifty miles away,
great snowy peaks rise up against the sky. To the north
and south and east all is endless wilderness — wilderness
of pine and prairie, of lake and stream — of all the vast
inanity of that moaning waste which sleeps between the
Bay of Hudson and the Rocky Mountains.*

*So far have we journeyed through that land; here we
shall rest awhile. The time of winter travel has drawn
to its close; the ice-road has done its work; the dogs may
lie down and rest; for those great snowy peaks are the
Rocky Mountains.*[11]

A few pages further, Butler speculated on the
nature of the terrain ahead, a land not yet seen.
Here, he undoubtedly revised and augmented
his account after returning from his journey.
Thus, while he appears to be wondering about
the future, in reality his foreshadowing is reportage of what he actually encountered: "Before
me lay a land of alps, a realm of mountain peaks
and gloomy cañons, where in countless valleys,
unseen by the eyes of man, this great Peace River
had its distant source."[12]

As with many travellers to the western mountains, the standards of comparison were the
European Alps. This reference was so common
as to be unremarkable. Even homebound readers were expected to frame a picture of the Alps
in their minds and compare it with the author's
depiction of the Rockies. Understandably,
very few accounts attempted to contrast North
American mountains with the lesser hills and
wildness existing in Great Britain.

In 1872, railroad engineer Sir Sandford
Fleming was given charge of a team surveying possible railroad routes across the Canadian

Rockies. In his account of the expedition, Fleming's secretary, George Monro Grant, a Glasgow-educated Canadian Presbyterian minister, noted that the clear western air made distances appear deceptively close. "The mountains ... stood in massive grandeur, thirty miles ahead, but on account of the morning light, in which every point came out clear, seemingly just on the other side of each new patch of wood or bit of prairie before us."[13]

Unlike Butler and Grant, an earlier traveller, Major Charles William Wilson, approached the Rockies from the west. As part of the British team on the international boundary survey between the United States and Canada, Wilson kept an extensive journal of his travels and explorations. While most of his group's work took place in the region between the Bitterroot Range and the Cascades, at one point they forged ahead to glimpse the mountains to the east beyond the Bitterroots:

Turning up to the left and following the Indian hunting trail, after a scramble over fallen timber and up a very steep ascent for about three miles, we at last reached the summit of the mountains and had a capital view of the pass and surrounding mountains. To the west we could see right up the pass through the Galton mountains and towards the east we could see the faint outline of the plains through the mouth of the rocky gorge that led to them. They are well called Rocky mountains, the range as far as we saw them being rugged peaks of bare rock of all shapes and sizes and many of them seemingly inaccessible....

Recognizing that there were more wonders ahead, Wilson and his party climbed higher still:

I went to the top of one of the peaks about 8,200 feet high with some of our party and we had a glorious view, a perfect sea of peaks all around us and running off to the north and south, whilst on the west we looked into the valley of the Flathead, small lakes of the most brilliant blue, with their borders of bright green herbage lay scattered in all directions in the hollows, hundreds of feet beneath us and (where it could still cling) some patches of snow and small glaciers heightened the beauty of the scene....[14]

That Butler and Wilson, both army officers, would dwell to such an extent on the scenic values of the mountains – Butler publicly in print and Wilson privately in his diary – indicates the extent of the change in sensibility that had taken place. Wilderness, it seems, had become less formidable and more mainstream.

Another who, like Wilson, started on the West Coast and travelled east was gold miner Richard Byron Johnson. He also remarked on the clearness of the British Columbia air: "In the far distance through these openings could be seen the snowy craggy summits of the Rocky Mountains. They could not have been less than from two to three hundred miles away; but in the marvelously clear atmosphere that exists in that part of America the distance did not look more than a quarter of what it really was. Behind us was a perfect chaos of mountain peaks trending away in all shapes and sizes to the verge of the horizon, where they gradually became indistinguishable from the light floating clouds that hovered about them."[15]

Travel Accounts for the Armchair

Richard Byron Johnson claimed to have struck it rich in British Columbia, and his book serves as a warning of the hardships of the miner's life as well as an entertaining travel account. It was just one of a large body of works on the North American West published in London by a multitude of publishers. There was, and still is, a substantial British audience for a literature on the American West.[16] The list of just one publisher – Low, Marston, Searle & Rivington – in 1879 included a number of travel works on the West by a wide spectrum of authors, including E. B. Tuttle, R. L. Price, W. H. G. Kingston, A. P. Vivian, and the previously cited Reverend G. M. Grant and Major W. F. Butler.[17] The same publisher later added western travel works by Lady Howard of Glossop, W. H. Russell, Edward Money, W. A. Baillie-Grohman, and John Mortimer Murphy; while R. B. Johnson was among its earlier authors.

The same firm also published works by the famed African explorer Henry Morton Stanley. Stanley's journalism career started when he began reporting on the Native "wars" in the American West. In 1867, Stanley climbed one peak of the Rockies for the view. "The summit of the hill is gained, and our eager eyes sweep over the view from the soaring peaks of the grand old 'Rockies,' which impress us as being impassable to further travel, down to their very base, where we see a gleaming stretch of river, and the scattered beginnings of a city [Denver] lying widely spread."[18]

Another well-known explorer, Sir Richard Burton, first saw the Rockies as he sped across the plains on his way to study the Mormons in Salt Lake City:

Presently ascending a little rise, we were shown for the first time a real bit of the far-famed Rocky Mountains, which was hardly to be distinguished from, except by a shade of solidity, the fleecy sunlit clouds resting upon the horizon: it was Frémont's Peak, the sharp, snow-clad apex of the Wind River Range.[19]

Burton's disappointment at this juncture equalled that of sporting journalist S. Nugent Townshend, who was initially disconcerted by his entry into the "Switzerland of America." Burton saved his effusion for South Pass, in contrast to the many who were less than impressed by it. He suggested that the pass epitomized the American way of things. At first, however, he contrasted it with both old world and new world landscapes:

*A pass it is not: it has some of the features of
Thermopylae or the Gorge of Killiecrankie; of the
European St. Bernard or Simplon; of the Alleghany
Passes or of the Mexican* Barrancas. *It is not, as it
sounds, a ghaut [gate] between lofty mountains, or,
as the traveler may expect, a giant gateway, opening
through Cyclopean walls of beetling rocks that rise in
forbidding grandeur as he passes onward to the Western
continent.*

Although South Pass did not have the form he
expected, at least in comparing it with other
mountain passes, Burton adjudges the name to be
meaningful in this particular place:

*And yet the word "Pass" has its significancy. In that
New World where nature has worked upon the larg-
est scale, where every feature of scenery, river and lake,
swamp and forest, prairie and mountain, dwarf their
congeners in the old hemisphere, this majestic level-
topped bluff, the highest steppe of the continent, upon
whose iron surface there is space enough for the armies
of the globe to march over, is the grandest and the most
appropriate of avenues.*[20]

Charles Wentworth Dilke, editor and later statesman, was hard on Burton's heels, although his
pilgrimage was more cultural in aim. His *Greater
Britain: A Record of Travel in English-Speaking
Countries During 1866 and 1867* was an effort to sig-
nify the underlying unity of England's scattered
offspring. This was of particular import because
relations between the United States and Britain
had been greatly strained by London's official
neutrality – which was seen as support for the
Confederacy – during the recently ended Civil
War. Nonetheless, Dilke was equally captured by
the Rocky Mountain scenery and its clear air:

View of Long's Peak. Arthur Pendarves Vivian. *Wanderings in
the Western Land* (1879). p. 126. Courtesy University of Idaho
Library.

*The view of the "Cordillera della Sierra Madre," the
Rocky Mountain main chain, from the outskirts of
Denver is sublime; that from the roof at Milan does not
approach it. Twelve miles from the city the mountains
rise abruptly from the Plains. Piled range above range
with step-like regularity, they are topped by a long
white line, sharply relieved against the indigo colour
of the sky. Two hundred and fifty miles of the mother
Sierra are in sight from our verandah; to the south,
Pike's Peak and Spanish Peak; Long's Peak to the
North; Mount Lincoln towering above all. The views
are limited only by the curvature of the earth, such is
the marvelous purity of the Coloradan air, the effect at
once of the distance from the sea and of the bed of limestone which underlies the Plains. The site of Denver is
heaven-blessed in climate as well as loveliness. The sky*

*is brilliantly blue, and cloudless from dawn till noon. In
the mid-day heats, cloud-making in the Sierra begins,
and by sunset the snowy chain is multiplied a hundred
times in curves of white and purple cumuli, while thunder rolls heavily along the range.*[21]

Dilke's description of the Rocky Mountains
from Denver is so definitive and prescriptive that
it is no wonder that Professor Lincoln Vanderbilt,
the self-proclaimed "Great American Traveller,"
borrowed quite heavily from it in his *New and
Wonderful Explorations*, which included, "the gorgeous scenery of the Rocky Mountains and the
Sierra Nevadas." In fact, it is likely that the entire
account is a plagiary. The first sentence from
Dilke's passage above becomes in Vanderbilt's
hand: "The view of the Cordillera della Sierra
Madre – the Rocky Mountain chain – from any
eminence in Denver, is sublime: that from the
roof of Milan cathedral does not nearly approach
it." Dilke's description of the mountains can
be contrasted with Vanderbilt's, "twelve miles
from the town the mountains rise in grandeur
indescribable abruptly from the broad plains,

piled range above range like a series of gigantic steps to heaven, topped by a long white line – the perpetual snowy range." Equally telling, however, is their common use of the word "heats" to describe the warmest part of the day. Throughout Vanderbilt's text is a sense of distance, of unreality, that makes the discovery of his plagiarism less surprising.[22]

Yet both Dilke and Vanderbilt were meeting the British public's need for information on the American West. As Oscar Wilde sardonically noted to a reporter in St. Louis, "We in England have no idea of the distances in your country. The impression there seems to be that all of the large cities are located in the suburbs of New York; then come the Rocky Mountains, next the Indians, then San Francisco and the ocean."[23]

Rails from Trails

By the time of Wilde's trip across the United States in 1882, the transcontinental railroad had opened up much of the American West to many British travellers. Canada's transcontinental route opened soon after but, as it happened, the routing choices did little to enhance the grandeur of approaching the Rockies. William Henry Grenfell Desborough, on a hunting expedition in 1888, dryly commented in his diary as his Canadian Pacific train left the plains, "... finally entering the Rockies: magnificent."[24] On the other hand, British politician John Edward Courtenay Bodley, writing in his diary the same year, had more enthusiasm for his railroad-supplied CPR notepad, calling it "a capital invention," than for his first view of the dramatic Canadian Rockies.[25]

The disappointment often expressed by rail passengers was particularly noted by novelist George Alfred Lawrence, whose visit to Utah was part of a scheme to encourage British investment in the heavily promoted Emma Silver Mine. His "champaign" is the flat, open countryside:

Travellers through many lands become familiar with disillusions: yet cannot I recall[l] such an imposture as these same Rocky Mountains, approached by railway from the east. From Omaha to Sherman, is all against the collar, but the rise is so gradual, that there seems no change in the dull champaign ; you are always looking at the same rim of low steep cliffs on the far horizon — at the same muddy creeks, weltering through stunted willows. You mount nine thousand feet above sea-level, without encountering as much broken ground as lies round Aldershot; and the grades, with very few exceptions, would be child's play to a skil[l]ful engineer.[26]

Maurice O'Connor Morris, in his pre-railroad *Rambles in the Rocky Mountains*, also expressed

disappointment while revealing how difficult it was to judge distances in the West: "They did not tower so far over their surrounding brethren as I expected, considering they are among the high points of the world; but I suppose we were nearly a hundred miles, if not more, from either."[27] Recognizing the disappointment, but thoughtful enough to identify the problem and propose a solution, was S. Nugent Townshend:

Indeed, we have all read so much about the easily accessible portions of the Rocky Mountains — which include only a very narrow fringe of their eastern base — that we are disposed to listen to the growls of the hundreds, and even thousands, who annually come to look at old Pike from his worst points of view, viz., those afforded from the railway-carriage windows, and generally from the eastern side. These people, if English, will tell you Pike is very inferior to Snowdon, to say nothing of the Alps; and Americans from New York or Pennsylvania will say, "Give me the White Mountains or the Alleghanies for real difficulty of ascent, and some sense of achievement when we get to the summit."

Mountains So Sublime

Townshend observes that these expressions derive from a very limited view of the western landscape. In short, those who denigrate the mountains have not yet experienced it.

People of this sort, in a mad six-hour rush along the base of the Rocky Mountains, previously to a mad fourteen hours' rush through them on the Union Pacific, forget that they have traversed only the flattest and easiest portions of the old Rockies, and not only go home knowing almost nothing of the magnificent scenery of these grand, massive, barren mountains, but with positively false and inverted notions of magnitudes that can only be seen and appreciated by long drives or runs over the mountain divisions of the Colorado Central from Denver, or from Pueblo over the Veta Pass in the mountain train of the Denver and Rio Grande. In fine, I have no patience with persons who, having had only the opportunity to see the back of a picture, will undertake the criticising of the details of its execution.[28]

Townshend was more charitable than most. Tourist Colon South was among the dis-appointed; he wrote that after "leaving Omaha, the train for a long distance traversed the prairie plains, and then commenced the gradual ascent of the outlying base of the Rocky Mountains. The gradient is so easy for a long distance, that the summit station at Sherman is reached almost imperceptibly. The ascent of the Rockies from the East is very tame and disappointing. When approaching the summit, some good views are obtained of distant mountain ranges covered with snow, but there was nothing very remarkably fine."[29] South felt that, for scenery, the western slope had more character than the eastern.

On descending the Rocky Mountains, towards the Pacific slope, the scenery is more interesting, grand, and romantic — mountains of rock, with snow-crowned peaks, tower one above another, in almost endless panoramas; masses of rugged, perpendicular, isolated rocks are scattered in every direction; tremendous ravines, spanned by light aerial bridges, which almost make one shudder to pass over them; yawning chasms, through which raging torrents dash foamingly along, while here

7. A PHOTOGRAPH BY BRITISH-BORN SALT LAKE
PHOTOGRAPHER C. R. SAVAGE IS THE SOURCE FOR THIS
VIEW OF THE RAILROAD'S ROUTE THROUGH UTAH.

Echo Cañon. C. R. Savage Photo. [76855] W. G. Marshall.
Through America; or, Nine Months in the United States. London,
Sampson Low, 1881. p. 140. Courtesy British Library.

*and there deep gorges skirt the railway, looking down
on rapids, surging and seething below. Sometimes
lovely canyons or valleys will be flanked on one side by
lofty cliffs with bold, steep escarpments, waterworn by
the storms of ages, and on the other with verdant hills
and grassy slopes, interspersed with bright, transpar-
ent rivers, now dashing merrily along, and now gently
meandering through beautiful green meadows in silent
grandeur.*[30]

But even coming from the west side, not all
were impressed. Perhaps this was a function of
the contrast. When going from east to west, the
Rockies appear as a wall at a great distance across
a nearly flat plain. From the other direction, one
rises gradually through successive mountain
ranges and that first view is primarily of just
slightly higher peaks. Isabella L. Bird noted at the
Sherman crossing that, "from this point eastward
the streams fall into the Atlantic. The ascent of
these apparently level plateaus is called 'crossing
the Rocky Mountains,' but I have seen nothing of the range, except for two peaks like teeth
lying low on the distant horizon."[31]

Another tourist, F. Barham Zincke, the Vicar
of Wherstead, south of Ipswich, also held his
yardstick up to the mountains and found them
deficient. It is likely that the vicar's complaint
about "scantily clothed" mountains and "naked"
rock reflects an earlier era's moral judgment.
Wilderness had only recently emerged from the
shadow of religious disapproval.

*The track from Shyenne [sic] to Denver lies along the
foot of the mountains, and is about one hundred and ten
miles in length. On your left is the boundless plain; on
your right are the mountains, rising suddenly like a wall
out of the plain. The first range is either scantily clothed*

with pine forests, or shows only the naked dark-coloured rock. Behind and above this is the snowy dividing ridge, which, however, in summer and autumn, has snow only on its highest peaks. In some places the lower range is of a bright red, as if the mountains were faced with red brick.[32]

South, Zincke, and other travellers use a common aesthetic language to deal with the immensity of the Rocky Mountains. Zincke thought that they fell short of the picturesque, while South found the descent on the Pacific side "romantic." A function of the eighteenth century's literary movements, these terms entered the language with specific meanings. But over time, the meanings shifted and merged towards something approaching general approbation.[33]

Nonetheless, especially for those not on the train, the sight of the Rocky Mountains marked a significant point on their journey, either as a divide or as a terminus. Of Canadian artist Paul Kane's expedition in 1846, he wrote: "October 30th – We had a fine view of the mountains from the boat for the first time; the men greeted them with a hearty cheer."[34] Similarly, George Grant, travelling with the Canadian railroad survey team, noted his group's celebration. "We stopped to drink to the Queen out of [the river's] clear ice-cold waters, and halted for dinner in a grove on the other side of it, thoroughly excited and awed by the grand forms that had begirt our path for the last three hours. We could sympathize with the enthusiast, who returned home after years of absence, and when asked what he had as an equivalent for so much lost time, – answered: 'I have seen the Rocky Mountains.'"[35]

Mountains So Sublime

2

British Travellers and Their Baggage

Met two parties of Britishers. English seem to be more plentiful than Americans out here.[1]

Who were these ubiquitous British travellers and what was it that brought them deep into the North American wilderness? Government agents, military or otherwise, were frequent travellers in the region, building roads, surveying railroad routes, or marking boundary lines. Official and unofficial reports of such projects were frequent and widely read. A few travellers represented financial interests, scouting out investment or immigration potentials. Among those were family outcasts or the second sons unable to inherit, the remittance men who at times settled the West with a particularly British flavour.[2] Some were purely tourists, sightseeing and jotting down observations on the landscape. Such tourists became more common after the opening of the transcontinental railroad, which eased travel and enhanced the available accommodations. Sportsmen formed another group of published authors, whose sometimes lyrical accounts of catching trout or shooting elk (called "wapiti") were potent symbols of their prowess. Journalists and authors were also members of the travelling class.

While authors have many reasons for recounting their adventures in print, all were contributing to a long tradition of British travellers' tales. The sheer number of such accounts – nearly three hundred publications on the West were counted by one historian[3] – was a function of technology as much as sociology. An increasingly literate audience in English-speaking countries, coupled with advances in the production of books and magazines, brought forth a deluge of literature on travel, as well as a host of other topics. The sub-genre "Travels in America" was a major tributary of that streaming flood.[4]

On the Boundary

At mid-century, at the closing of the fur-trade era, many of the British travellers to the inland North American West were government officials and army officers. Charles William Wilson and John Keast Lord were members of the British Boundary Commission, charged with marking the boundary from Lake of the Woods to Vancouver Island along the 49th parallel. Wilson's diaries were not published for another hundred years, but naturalist Lord generated several books out of his experiences, the best known being *The Naturalist in Vancouver Island and British Columbia*, which was published in two volumes in 1866.[5]

British naval officer Richard C. Mayne and Royal Engineer H. Spencer Palmer mapped and surveyed the interior of British Columbia in the late 1850s. Reports of their explorations were submitted to the *Journal of the Royal Geographical Society*, and appeared in print in 1861.[6] These reports are seldom descriptive of the scenery; although some things are touted as "pretty," they are purposefully dry and scientific. This lack of descriptive language for the new world scenery is a function of the publishing venue. Scientific disciplines, such as geology, geography, and natural history, depend upon compartmentalization through naming, reports of observable phenomena, and repeatability. Thus by its nature, a scientific report, particularly one to the *Journal of the Royal Geographical Society*, would

tend to avoid the subjective observations of the picturesque landscape. In another such report to the Royal Geographical Society in 1868, Alfred P. Waddington, former Superintendent of Schools in the growing British colony of British Columbia and proponent of the transcontinental railroad, permits himself a scenic reference in describing an area near the mouth of the Quesnelle River. He commented, "The plain itself (the only one in British Columbia of any extent) has been admired by all who have seen it, on account of its vast pasturages and park-like scenery."[7]

Once the boundary between Canada and the United States was established, the forces pushing for Confederation promised British Columbia that a northern transcontinental railroad would be built. Waddington, as part of his report to the Royal Geographical Society, urged the rapid construction of a railroad across Canada to keep British trade British and to keep the lines of communication open with Asia in the case of war with the United States.[8] As part of this process, engineer Sir Sandford Fleming was charged with

8. MAJOR BUTLER USING THE ICE ROAD OF THE
SASKATCHEWAN RIVER.

The "Forks" of the Saskatchewan. William Francis Butler.
*The Great Lone Land: A Narrative of Travel and Adventure in
the North-West of America* ([1891?]). opp. p. 329. Courtesy
University of Idaho Library.

surveying a route across Canada, and particularly across the Canadian Rockies. The expedition's secretary, George Monro Grant, a Presbyterian minister from Nova Scotia, kept a journal that he turned into *Ocean to Ocean; Sandford Fleming's Expedition through Canada in 1872.*[9] Another 1872 journal was maintained by the Howse Pass survey team's commissariat, former British Army Sergeant R. M. Rylatt, which he transcribed for his children in 1885. Remaining in the family, it was not published until 1991.[10]

Also in 1872, but later in the season, army major William F. Butler decided to strike out on his own to find the easiest railroad crossing in the Canadian Rockies. After his earlier service

in the plains of western Canada he wrote about his winter expedition to Rocky Mountain House in *The Great Lone Land* (1872).[11] Returning to London, he had hoped to join the quasi-military expedition sponsored by the Royal Geographical Society to search for Dr. David Livingstone in Africa. To his dismay, it was the navy rather than the army that was selected for the journey. In any event, this effort was overshadowed by journalist Henry M. Stanley's successful trek to locate the missing missionary. Disappointed in his efforts to join the search, Butler returned to Canada. The account of his second cross-country winter trek, *The Wild Northland, Being the Story of a Winter Journey, with Dogs, across Northern North America*, is riveting reading; along with the usual hazards of wilderness travel, he had to deal with the extreme cold, snow, and ice.[12]

In his 1911 autobiography, posthumously published, Butler asserted that his two winter expeditions across Canada were merely the result of intemperate bursts of exploring enthusiasm.[13] The earlier accounts show clearly, however, that these were instead extreme efforts to demonstrate his military competence because he lacked funds to purchase an officer's commission. In this effort he was ultimately successful, later serving in Africa and attaining the rank of Lieutenant General in the British Army.

Financing the West

Among those crossing the mountains for financial reasons was prominent London lawyer Wallis Nash, who visited Oregon in 1877 to investigate opportunities for settlement and investment in the western lands. Nash was particularly interested in a scheme to use British pounds to build a railroad from Yaquina Bay on the Pacific Ocean across Oregon to the Snake River. He was much pleased by what he found, and when personal circumstances offered the possibility, he emigrated, transplanting himself and his family to a farm in the Willamette Valley. The account of his first trip, *Oregon: There and Back in 1877*, was thus followed by a sequel in 1882 entitled *Two Years in Oregon*.[14]

British capitalism, like federal largess, played a major role in the development of the American West. Extractive industries, often funded by overseas capital, dominated western life, culture, and politics. The sale of mining claims and stocks not only fostered the development of the West but also provided an opportunity for some to pocket British gold. Colon South found the importunate mining promoters quite a nuisance during his 1883 mountain holiday.[15] In 1873, George Alfred Lawrence, author of the popular novel *Guy Livingstone*, published an account of his trip to "Silverland," the silver mines of Utah. Besides being a descriptive account of a journey to the Rocky Mountain frontier, the volume also served as a promotional tool for the officers of the Emma Silver Mining Company.[16] The subsequent failure of the firm amidst charges of fraud could not be laid to Lawrence, yet his account surely persuaded some British investors to drop many pounds sterling down a Utah mine shaft.[17]

Another minor literary figure, the poet James Thomson – not the James Thomson who wrote "The Seasons" but the James Thomson known as "B. V." who wrote "The City of Dreadful Night" – spent from May to December of 1872 as secretary of the Champion Gold and Silver Mines Company of Colorado. In this role, he acted as on-site agent for British investors. His diary and memorandum book from this period, as well as other papers, were collected by his friend and publisher Bertram Dobell and placed in the Bodleian Library, Oxford. The memorandum book is entirely devoted to Thomson's efforts to get the mine productive despite an unscrupulous mine superintendent. As well, the more personal diary contains a close account of his travels throughout the mountains, often on foot, and includes vignettes of the people he met, weather he experienced, books he read, and scenery he exalted.[18]

Colorado also drew capitalist Allayne Beaumont Legard who toured the territory in the early 1870s to seek out investment and business opportunities. Writing for private circulation, Legard was so taken with the mountain scenery at one point that he stopped his horse to make, "a few notes of its description in my pocket-book as I went along." Yet later he judged Colorado, taken as a whole, to be "the most barren part of the United States I have seen, and, with the exception of some of the sandy heaths round Aldershot, the worst land I have ever come across."[19]

Tourists and Sightseers

While Isabella L. Bird, graduating from the rank of tourist to travel writer, could remark of the Colorado Rockies, "this is no region for tourists and women;" tourists were, and still are, drawn to the scenery of the North American West.[20] Her observation was, of course, refuted by her own travels in the mountains. Like Bird, many of the Britons who visited the West had previously visited other parts of the world, particularly Europe, and were not averse to drawing comparisons.

Isabella Bird travelled from the West Coast to Colorado in 1873 for her health. She had been to, and loved, the Sandwich, or Hawaiian, Islands, but she found immense beauty in the Colorado Rockies. Her ill health seemed to disappear once she got out-of-doors and onto a horse. In spite of her protestations that the Rocky Mountains were not fit for tourists and women, she revelled in the beauty and the sense of freedom she found in the West. She wrote, almost upon arrival in California:

I have found a dream of beauty at which one might look all one's life and sigh. Not lovable, like the Sandwich Islands, but beautiful in its own way! A strictly North American beauty – snow-splotched mountains, huge pines, red-woods, sugar pines, silver spruce; a crystalline atmosphere, waves of the richest color; and a pine-hung lake which mirrors all beauty on its surface.[21]

Later, in Colorado, finally more accepting of the grandeur of the western landscape, she added: "I have written that this scenery is not lovable, but I love it."[22]

It was the railroad that opened up the West to a larger number of tourists and the railroad companies were quick to market the western scenery to potential visitors.[23] The western scenery could be overwhelming, however. Politician John E. C. Bodley, travelling on the Canadian Pacific in 1888, wrote in his diary: "Not yet weary of scenery I opened the windows of the car and for nearly two hours there passed before me a wonderful panorama." However, it all proved to be too much, and he added, "My eyes were getting quite weary of scenery and it was almost a relief after passing through the canyons of the Chilliwack to emerge into a comparatively level tract on the banks of the Columbia at Revelstoke."[24]

Rudyard Kipling planned his 1889 visit to the United States as part of his journey from India to literary fame in London. Articles he wrote on his cross-country train trip from west to east for an Indian newspaper were pirated by American publishers and snapped up by an American public, eager to see what the famous author had to say about them. Kipling may not have been complimentary about Americans in general, but he did find something to admire in the western landscape:

Then the scenery began – poured forth with the reckless profusion of Nature, who when she wants to be amiable succeeds only in being oppressively magnificent. The [Columbia] river was penned between gigantic stone walls crowned with the ruined bastions of Oriental palaces. The stretch of green water widened and was guarded by pine-clad hills three thousand feet high. A wicked devil's thumb nail of rock shot up a hundred feet in midstream. A sand-bar of blinding white sand gave promise of flat country that the next bend denied; for lo! we were running under a triple tier of fortification, lava-topped, pine-clothed, and terrible. Behind them the white dome of Mount Hood ran fourteen thousand feet into the blue, and at their feet the river threshed among a belt of cottonwood trees.[25]

Like Bodley, Kipling had second thoughts: "I was surfeited with scenery. There is a great deal in the remark of the discontented traveller: 'When you have seen a fine forest, a bluff, a river, and a lake you have seen all the scenery of western America. Sometimes the pine is three hundred feet high, and sometimes the rock is, and sometimes the lake is a hundred miles long.

But it is all the same, don't you know. I'm getting sick of it.' I dare not say getting sick. I'm only tired. If providence could distribute all this beauty in little bits where people most wanted it – among you in India, – it would be well. But it is en masse, overwhelming, with nobody but the tobacco chewing captain of a river steamboat to look at it."[26]

Kipling made a side trip into Yellowstone Park and summed it up as "a howling wilderness of three thousand square miles, full of all imaginable freaks of a fiery nature." He added: "I have been through Yellowstone National Park in a buggy, in the company of an adventurous old lady from Chicago and her husband, who disapproved of the scenery as being 'ongodly.' I fancy it scared them."[27] Here Kipling slyly contradicts the idea that American wilderness, in all its sublimity, was a true manifestation of God's works and thus wielded a mystical power that European scenery could not match.[28]

Some, such as Charles Russell, later Lord Chief Justice of England, did their touring on the side as part of some other activity, perhaps a business junket. Russell visited Montana in 1883 for the Northern Pacific's completion ceremony there. Unlike Kipling, Russell skipped Yellowstone Park, but complained in his diary of the lack of rail transportation into California's Yosemite.[29]

An earlier tourist on a vacation trip, although less of a descriptive writer than Bird or Kipling, was F. Barham Zincke, the Vicar of Wherstead and Chaplain in Ordinary to the Queen. In his *Last Winter in the United States, Being Table-Talk Collected during a Tour Through the Late Southern Confederation, the Far West, the Rocky Mountains &c.* he merely noted that the "mountains are close upon [Denver], and present a view that is very grand."[30]

Sports and Sportsmen

A smaller contingent of writing Britons travelling to the West was composed of sportsmen; to the sports aficionado, the story of the hunt was as important as the experience. Those who fished in the West's streams or hunted in its forests found rich game resources and incomparable scenery.[31] Rudyard Kipling went fly fishing for trout in both Washington and Montana. He found the Yellowstone River:

… alive with trout. It was. I fished it from noon til twilight, and the fish bit at the brown hook as though never a fat trout-fly had fallen on the water. From pebbly reaches, quivering in the heat-haze where the foot caught on stumps cut four-square by the chisel-tooth of the beaver; past the fringe of the water-willow crowded with the breeding trout-fly and alive with toads and water-snakes; over the drifted timber to the grateful shadow of the big trees that darkened the holes where the fattest fish lay, I worked for seven hours. The mountain flanks on either side of the valley gave back the heat as the desert gives it, and the dry sand by the railway track, where I found a rattlesnake, was hot-iron to the touch.[32]

It wasn't just the hunt that drew sportsmen. As cattle entrepreneur Moreton Frewen described it to his fiancée, "the sporting instinct implies a great deal beyond *killing*. The love of new &

wild experiences, the artist soul, [and] the love of untutored nature." As an avid outdoorsman, Frewen hosted large parties of aristocratic hunters at his immense ranch in Wyoming.[33]

Of the sportsmen, the most remarkable was William Adolph Baillie-Grohman, who wrote for a number of British journals about big-game hunting. Beginning in 1879 he turned from Europe's game and sought trophy heads throughout Colorado, Wyoming, Idaho, Montana, and British Columbia.[34] Although his genealogy included Austrian aristocracy and ties to the Duke of Wellington, he disdained the pampered life of many European sportsmen. He identified three ways to hunt in the Rockies. First was the method used by so-called "top-shelfers," featuring servants, guns for all occasions, and London's best outfitting. The second involved travel to lonely army bases where, he discovered, the officers would gladly leave their monotonous duties to organize a hunting trip with such a cultured companion. Third was to attach oneself to a group of trappers and hire their services as guides, cooks, and outfitters. They would

continue to trap but, by providing a base camp, would leave one free to hunt. Compared to the other methods, this method was the most inexpensive and effective; its main drawback, Baillie-Grohman noted, was having to deal with the American frontiersman as an equal.[35]

The "top-shelfer" mode of hunting was the most common, particularly among the aristocrats. J. S. Campion related an embarrassing encounter with such a hunting party in a Leavenworth, Kansas hotel around 1879. Asking about an overwhelming pile of London baggage, he was told by the desk clerk, "Tell you what's up? There is a parcel of English *a-ristocrats* arrived, who are going to kill all the game in the country. They have brought their dogs, their weapons, and their mountebanks with them, and they have got a kit of everything in the universal world that is of no earthly use in this country. They are in No. 8, and there is nothing good enough for them in this 'blarsted hotel!'" Campion's generous offer to assist the hunting party was rudely spurned because he had not been properly introduced.[36] Kipling had a similar

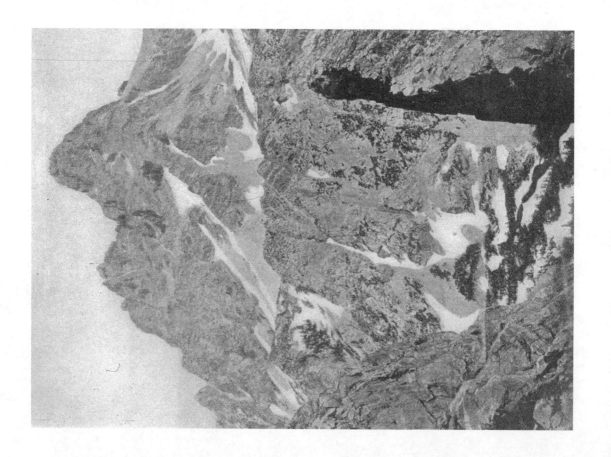

encounter with a "young English idiot I met
knocking about in his high collars, attended by
a valet [who] condescended to tell me that 'you
can't be too careful who you talk to in these
parts,' and stalked on, fearing, I suppose, every
minute for his social chastity."[37]

The conflicts between the Americans' easy-
going assumption of equality and the Britons'
strong sense of class and standing, particularly in
the West, were epitomized in Campion's experience. Baillie-Grohman tells of an "amusing inci-
dent" where an English sportsman's impromptu
American valet, fed up with the continual
patronizing, emphatically quit his job by shooting his Lordship's portable bathtub full of holes.[38]

Baillie-Grohman also turned entrepreneur
and pioneer, trying to establish an agricultural empire in eastern British Columbia on a
government land grant, before giving up and
returning to Europe. Had his irrigation scheme
been successful, he undoubtedly would have
followed Wallis Nash's path and forsaken the
old world for the new. Another hunter with an
entrepreneurial streak was Windham Thomas
Wyndham-Quin, the Fourth Earl of Dunraven.
After observing the abounding sportsmen and
the clearly declining game in the early 1870s,
he purchased 6,600 acres in Estes Park[39] north
of Denver as a big game hunting enclave. Lord
Dunraven built a large tourist hotel there but bad
weather, squatters, poachers, and local antago-
nisms put an end to his western estate; nearly ten
years later he sold out. This estate is now part of
Rocky Mountain National Park.[40] In later years,
he remembered most vividly the distinct and
vibrant colours of the American West. Moreton
Frewen's nephew, Shane Leslie, reported that the
old man had lost nothing of his literary style:
"His memory of the sunsets in the Rockies will

IO. CALLED A PARK, THIS VALLEY IN COLORADO
REMINDED MANY TRAVELLERS OF MORE MANICURED
BRITISH LANDSCAPES.

The Black Canon and Range in Estes Park. Arthur Pendarves
Vivian. *Wanderings in the Western Land* (1879). p. 138. Courtesy
University of Idaho Library.

serve the modern traveller yet, for there are
unchangeable aspects of American life. He used
to compare the virulent reds and yellows turning
to a pallor of green and mauve on the mountains
to the blood passing out of the face of a dying
man."[41]

Sportsmen came in all varieties, but there were
certain commonalities: they were all rich enough
to afford the travel across the Atlantic, the train
trip across the country, and the hire of an outfit,
not to mention the cost of shipping their trophies
home. John Turner-Turner was clearly among
this group during his first two hunting trips, to
Virginia in September 1883 and to Wyoming

in August 1884, where he stopped for a visit at
Moreton Frewen's Powder River ranch. Yet his
third trip, to British Columbia in April 1886,
was the result, he wrote, of the collapse of his
financial exchequer. Accompanied by his long-
suffering wife, "his constant companion during
these travels," whom he identified only as "L.,"
Turner spent two years hunting and trapping
furs under quite meagre conditions, both winter
and summer, before returning to England in June
of 1888.[42]

In the News

As a journalist covering the military conquest
of the Plains Indians in late 1867, Henry Morton
Stanley impressed his New York editors suffi-
ciently that they sent him off to find the missing
African explorer Dr. David Livingstone and,
incidentally, add to the paper's readership. He did
very little exploring in the Rockies, declaring at
one point that they seemed "impassable to fur-

ther travel."[43] In his autobiography, Stanley later recalled that as an orphan in Wales he overheard tavern drinkers singing "To the West, where the mighty Mizzourah," and this "gave us the vision of a wide and free land awaiting the emigrant, and an enormous river flowing between silent shores to the sea." We may well wonder whether this was what drew him across the Atlantic as a cabin boy and urged him to jump ship in New Orleans. Nor does Stanley explicitly connect this childhood experience to his newspaper career that had its start where the "Mizzourah" meets the Rockies, in the upper plains region of the West.[44]

Other British journalists in the West included Francis Francis, who wrote for *Nineteenth Century* and later tried a novel about New Mexico; S. N. Townshend, who wrote for *The Field* under the sobriquet "St. Kames;" and *Athenaeum* editor Charles W. Dilke, who made a trip around the world in 1866 and 1867.[45] Some of the sportsmen, Baillie-Grohman among them, also contributed their hunting stories to periodicals.

Fellow Travellers

While a multitude of Britons came out to the West and returned home to write about their adventures, it is often difficult to determine why they undertook such an arduous journey. For Richard Burton, a secular sort of pilgrim, the opportunity to visit Salt Lake City was as important as his earlier exploration of the holy city of Mecca:[46] Robert Louis Stevenson, on the other hand, travelled by emigrant train to the woman he loved in California.[47] And Oscar Wilde, the champion of the new aesthetics, was on a moneymaking lecture tour, speaking in opera houses and recital halls throughout the United States.[48]

The reasons for travelling were many, with health, financial gain, sport, and curiosity most often mentioned. Together, they compose a distinctive and forceful picture of the North American West at a time of great physical and cultural change. British travellers, in their books, articles, diaries, and photographs, documented the North American West's growing pains; when

Mountains So Sublime

the mountains were swept of game, the forests logged for mining timbers, and the prairies emptied of buffalo. The cultural landscape was changing as well. America was becoming a world power; the economic dream of the era was manifest in Mark Twain's phrase, "the Gilded Age."[49] Native Americans were forced onto reservations and thousands of acres were opened up to homesteaders who followed the Jeffersonian agrarian ideal only to be thrust back to the cities by uncompromising "Nature" and even less charitable capitalists. Throughout it all, the English tourist and traveller wandered, taking notes and impressions to feed the insatiable curiosity about the strange lands in the West.

3

Literary Travellers

Honoured with your special commission, I at once hurried across to Denver, and thence still westward until I found myself among the big vertebrae of this longish backbone of America.[1]

Many British travellers who visited the American West during the late nineteenth century were authors, poets, and journalists. Some familiar names are Rudyard Kipling, Robert Louis Stevenson, Oscar Wilde, Henry Morton Stanley, and James Thomson; the latter found himself among the "big vertebrae." The impact of the western landscape on their life and work was at times profound, although it often took a back seat to their observations on the denizens of the West. As a tourist, Kipling visited the wonders of Yellowstone Park, and remarked on both the scenery and his fellow travellers. Stevenson crossed the continent by emigrant train to join his future wife in California. Wilde, on a lecture tour spreading the doctrine of aestheticism, called the Rocky Mountains, "perhaps the most beautiful part of the West."[2] Stanley's vantage from a peak overlooking the Colorado Rockies urged him to proclaim the coming greatness of America. Thomson, the poet of depression, spent a nearly idyllic season in the Rockies, jotting descriptions of the landscape in his pocket journal. It was, wrote one biographer, "one of the

pleasantest episodes of his career."[3] Each writer added to the growing literature on the landscape of the American West.

Isn't She a Daisy?

Rudyard Kipling's brash account of his American tour has its own bizarre subtext. Kipling gained experience and notoriety writing satiric observations on Indian politicians and government officials for the *Allahabad* (India) *Pioneer*. His editor, hoping for a reprieve from his angry readers, sent him to America in 1889. The twenty-three year old Kipling took this opportunity to return to England where he thought (correctly) that his literary gifts would be appreciated. His contrary crossing of the American continent, from west to east, was recorded in a series of articles published in the *Pioneer*. Within a few years, these articles were collected into book form and pirated by American publishers for an American audience, against Kipling's wishes. "Protect me from the wrath of an outraged community," he wrote, "if these letters be ever read by American eyes."[4] His rude comments on the Americans were widely denounced and widely read, and he was forced to protect his copyright and pocketbook by issuing an authorized American edition in 1899.[5]

After landing in San Francisco and lounging about with the rich merchants and poor artists who were members of the Bohemian Club, taking the required tour of Chinatown, and pursuing a study of saloon lunches, Kipling took the train to Portland, Oregon. On his way north, his admiration for Bret Harte's California was strengthened as he viewed the passing landscape:

At six in the morning the heat was distinctly unpleasant, but seeing with the eye of the flesh that I was in Bret Harte's own country, I rejoiced. There were the pines and madrone clad hills his miners lived and fought among; there was the heated red earth that showed whence gold had been washed; the dry gulch, the red, dusty road where Hamblin was used to stop the stage in the intervals of his elegant leisure and superior card-play; there was the timber felled and sweating resin in the sunshine; and, above all, there was the quivering pungent heat that Bret Harte drives into your dull brain with the magic of his pen.[6]

From Portland, he made an excursion up the Columbia River by steamboat. His companion said: "Say, young feller, we're going to see some scenery now. You shout and sing." And soon his new friend was "dancing on the fore-deck shouting, 'Isn't she a daisy? Isn't she a darling?' He had found a waterfall – a blown thread of white vapor that broke from the crest of a hill – a waterfall eight hundred and fifty-feet high whose voice was even louder than the voice of the river."[7] It was not until after that point, he thought, that "the scenery began." The swift and still unchecked Columbia constrained between steeply rising rocky bluffs was evidence of "oppressively magnificent" Nature.[8]

After a night in a rude hotel at The Dalles, Kipling hurried back to Portland to go fishing on the Clackamas River. Like many of today's travellers in the West, he was surprised that it was possible to "sit in a bedizened bar-room furnished with telephone and [stock] clicker, and in

half an hour be in the woods."[9] The fishing trip was a huge success. The group caught sixteen fish for a grand total of 142 pounds; except for the first three, all were weighed and returned to the river.[10]

From Portland, Kipling proceeded to booming Tacoma, newly burnt Seattle, sturdy Vancouver, and extremely British Victoria. It was on the return to Tacoma by steamboat that he exclaimed that he was already "surfeited with scenery" yet he had barely left the coast.[11] Taking the Northern Pacific from Tacoma, Kipling found the bare hills of the east side of the

Cascades gloomy and depressing compared with similar sites in India:

Night was falling when we cleared the forests and sailed out upon a wilderness of sage brush. The desolations on Montgomery, the wilderness of Sind, the hummock-studded desert of Bikaneer, are joyous and homelike compared to the impoverished misery of the sage. It is blue, it is stunted, it is dusty. It wraps the rolling hills as a mildewed shroud wraps the body of a long-dead man. It makes you weep from sheer loneliness, and there is no getting away from it.[12]

Up the Rockies to Livingston, Montana, the northern entrance to Yellowstone Park, Kipling hurried, making comments on American tourists and their attitude to the landscape. Before entering the park, he put in another bout of fishing, spending seven hours in the Yellowstone River beside the railroad tracks. On the stagecoach to the park, the tourists were rapturous, while Kipling was struck by their indifference to the perilous journey. The scenery in Yellowstone

Park's "howling wilderness" was, according to the American tourists, "elegant." Kipling, fearing for his life on the narrow mountain track, asked himself, "what 'elegance' lies in a thousand-foot pile of honey-colored rock, riven into peak and battlement, the highest peak defiantly crowned by an eagle's nest, the eaglet peering into the gulf and screaming for his food, I could not for the life of me understand. But they speak a strange tongue."[13]

Perhaps "elegant" was the wrong word. Kipling thought at first that Yellowstone Park was going to be beyond his powers of description. It took him three rewrites, of which the first two were torn up "fearing lest those across the water should say that I had gone mad on a sudden."[14] His tour of the park started at Mammoth Hot Springs where he found two British subjects serving in the U.S. Army guarding the scenery from the tourists. Then he was off to Norris Geyser Basin, the Firehole River, Hell's Half Acre, Riverside Geyser, Old Faithful, Beehive and Turban Geysers, the Giantess, Castle Geyser, Mary's Lake, and the Grand Canyon of the Yellowstone. From the edge of the chasm, he wrote that it was twice as marvellous as scenes in India:

*All I can say is that without warning or preparation
I looked into a gulf seventeen hundred feet deep with
eagles and fish-hawks circling far below. And the sides
of that gulf were one wild welter of color – crimson,
emerald, cobalt, ochre, amber, honey splashed with port-
wine, snow-white, vermilion, lemon, and silver-gray,
in wide washes. The sides did not fall sheer, but were
graven by time and water and air into monstrous heads
of kings, dead chiefs, men and women of the old time.
So far below that no sound of its strife could reach us,*

the Yellowstone River ran – a finger-wide strip of jade-green. The sunlight took those wondrous walls and gave fresh hues to those that nature had already laid there. Once I saw the dawn break over a lake in Rajputana and the sun set over the Oody Sagar amid a circle of the Holman hills. This time I was watching both performances going on below me – upside down you understand – and the colors were real![15]

From Yellowstone Park, he proceeded by rail to Salt Lake City, where, after comparing Mormon polygamy to that found in India, Kipling found the valley, "very fair. Bench after bench of land, flat as a table against the flanks of the ringing hills, marks where the Salt Lake rested for a while as it sunk from an inland sea to a lake fifty miles long and thirty broad." He added, prophetically, "Before long the benches will be covered with houses."[16]

Back on the train to Denver, through the Gunnison River Gorge, whose twisted route took up many paragraphs of type in the guidebooks of the time. Kipling, as usual, was more concerned with the safety of the engineering.

13–14. THE NATURAL WONDERS OF YELLOWSTONE PARK, LIKE MAMMOTH HOT SPRINGS (RIGHT) AND UPPER FIRE HOLE (FOLLOWING PAGE), CONTINUE TO BE GREAT TOURIST ATTRACTIONS.

right: Mammoth Hot Springs. Windham Thomas Dunraven, Earl of Wyndham-Quin, 1841–1926. *The Great Divide: Travels in the Upper Yellowstone in the Summer of 1874* (1876). opp. p. 340. Courtesy University of Idaho Library.

following page: Upper Fire Hole. Windham Thomas Dunraven, Earl of Wyndham-Quin, 1841–1926. *The Great Divide: Travels in the Upper Yellowstone in the Summer of 1874* (1876). opp. p. 291. Courtesy University of Idaho Library.

We had been climbing for very many hours, and attained a modest elevation of some seven or eight thousand feet above the sea, when we entered a gorge, remote from the sun, where the rocks were two thousand feet sheer, and where a rock-splintered river roared and howled ten feet below a track which seemed to have been built on the simple principle of dropping miscellaneous dirt into the river and pinning a few rails atop. There was a glory and a wonder and a mystery about that mad ride which

Mountains So Sublime

I felt keenly (you will find it properly dressed up in the guide-books), until I had to offer prayers for the safety of the train. There was no hope of seeing the track two hundred yards ahead. We seemed to be running into the bowels of the earth at the invitation of an irresponsible stream. Then the solid rock would open and disclose a curve of awful twistfulness.[17]

Over some more rugged country to Denver, then Omaha and Chicago, Kipling left the West as abruptly as he entered, hurrying on to London. He did travel to the United States again in 1896 after his marriage to an American woman, and spent a year in Vermont before returning to England to receive his 1907 Nobel Prize. For the remainder of his life, Kipling volunteered as the principal defender of the fading memory of the late Queen's Empire.

Grateful Mountain Feeling

Robert Louis Stevenson was born in Edinburgh in 1850, and studied engineering (like his father), and then law. By the time he took a trip to the United States in 1879, he was an accomplished travel writer with two books published. He had met, in France, a married American woman with grown children, and had fallen in love with her. Against the wishes of his family and friends, he followed her back to California. To save money, he travelled as an emigrant, though not quite steerage class, both aboard ship and then by train across the United States. His lady love's divorce and a substantial allowance from his father, with whom he had finally reconciled, meant that they could get married and settle down in a former mining camp in the hills north of San Francisco.[18]

Although ill and weak during much of the transcontinental journey, Stevenson managed to include some memorable passages about the landscape of the American West. Of the far western plains and its low foothills he wrote with little enjoyment or enthusiasm:

To cross such a plain is to grow home-sick for the mountains. I longed for the Black Hills of Wyoming, which I knew we were soon to enter, like an ice-bound whaler

15. BASED ON A PHOTOGRAPH BY SAN FRANCISCO
PHOTOGRAPHER CARLETON E. WATKINS, THIS SCENE
OF THE SIERRA ILLUSTRATES THE VIEW FROM THE
RAILROAD.

American River Cañon. C.E. Watkins Photo. [76854]
W. G. Marshall. *Through America; or, Nine Months in the United States*. London, Sampson Low, 1881. p. 254. Courtesy British Library.

for the spring. Alas! And it was a worse country than the other. All Sunday and Monday we travelled through these sad mountains, or over the main ridge of the Rockies, which is a fair match to them for misery of aspect. Hour after hour it was the same unhomely and unkindly world about our onward path; tumbled boulders, cliffs that drearily imitate the shape of monuments and fortifications – how drearily, how tamely, none can tell who has not seen them; not a tree, not a patch of sward, not one shapely or commanding mountain form; sage-brush, eternal sage-brush; over all, the same weariful and gloomy colouring, greys warming into brown, greys darkening toward black; and for sole sign of life, here and there a few fleeing antelopes; here

and there, but at incredible intervals, a creek running in a cañon. The plains have a grandeur of their own; but here there is nothing but a contorted smallness. Except for the air, which was light and stimulating, there was not one good circumstance in that God-forsaken land.[19]

Traversing the inland desert beyond a small corner of Utah, which "leaves no particular impressions on the mind," Stevenson's train headed into the Sierras.[20] After the "desolate and desert scenes, fiery hot and deadly weary," Stevenson awakened in the mountains. "It was a clear, moonlit night; but the valley was too narrow to admit the moonshine direct, and only a diffused glimmer whitened the tall rocks and relieved the blackness of the pines. A hoarse clamour filled the air; it was the continuous plunge of a cascade somewhere near at hand among the mountains. The air struck chill, but tasted good and vigorous in the nostrils – a fine, dry, old mountain atmosphere. I was dead sleepy, but I returned to roost with a grateful mountain feeling at my heart."[21] The welcoming mountain scenery "was like meeting one's wife. I had come home again – home from unsightly deserts to the green and habitable corners of the earth."[22] Perhaps this metaphor came to mind because of his planned meeting with the woman who was to become his bride.

In May 1880, Stevenson and Fanny Osbourne were married in San Francisco and quickly moved to the clear air of Mount St. Helena, where they "squatted" at Silverado, the site of an old silver mine. Here they made a brief home in the hills while Stevenson continued writing.

Stevenson's affinity with the mountain landscape permeates *The Silverado Squatters*, his account of their stay at the mine. It starts, "The scene of this little book is on a high mountain." It is, he says, "the Mont Blanc of one section of the California Coast range."[23] Later, he adds, "there was something satisfactory in the sight of that great mountain that enclosed us to the north: whether it stood robed in sunshine, quaking to its topmost pinnacle with the heat and brightness of the day; or whether it set itself to weaving vapours, wisp after wisp growing, trembling, fleeting, and fading the blue."[24] While much of the book deals with making a home out of an abandoned mining camp's bunkhouse, it is the descriptions of the landscape that charm the reader. Most expressive of all is his chapter on "The Sea Fogs." Awakening early one day, he saw a new and different landscape in the bright morning sunshine. "Napa Valley was gone; gone were all the lower slopes and woody foothills of the range; and in their place, not a thousand feet below me, rolled a great level ocean."[25] This ocean of fog lingered a good part of the morning and provided Stevenson with extensive opportunities for description and comparison.

By July of 1880, however, the Stevenson family had left for the British Isles and, eventually, Samoa. His reminiscences of California, it is claimed, contributed the landscape to *Treasure Island* (1883) and to other works.[26]

So Vast its Size

Born in Ireland in October 1854 and christened Oscar Fingal O'Flahertie Wills Wilde, Oscar

Wilde was twenty-seven years of age when he arrived in New York to begin a lecture tour. The genesis of the tour was less than auspicious. Wilde had become the exemplar of a fading social fad, and his contemporaries, a group of what could only be called foppish young men, had been satirized and caricatured in *Punch Magazine* and roundly burlesqued by Gilbert and Sullivan in *Patience* for Richard D'Oyly Carte's opera company. The foppish young men included the Pre-Raphaelite Brotherhood, with members such as critic William Michael Rossetti and his brother, the artist, Dante Gabriel Rossetti. D'Oyly Carte, in a master stroke of publicity, persuaded Wilde, by the offer of greatly needed financial remuneration, to speak on aestheticism in the United States in 1882 as part of the promotion for his New York production of *Patience*.[27]

More of a public figure than a successful author, although he had published a small book of poetry, Wilde agreed to address American audiences on the Pre-Raphaelite ideals, called by D'Oyly Carte's American publicist "this latest form of fashionable madness."[28] He was feted,

wined, and dined on the East Coast – including an evening at the home of American travel writer A. A. Hayes, whose book of travels in Colorado had appeared two years earlier – and then undertook the crossing of the continent.

Wilde's route was circuitous. New York was first, then Philadelphia, Washington, Boston, and Chicago, not counting intermediate stops. From there he went through the middle states and then to California and back, stopping for a series of lectures in Utah and Colorado. He wrote to his London friends about the Mormon polygamists in the Salt Lake City audience, and of his descent into a Leadville silver mine to drink whiskey with the miners.[29] That he acted the part of the foppish "dude" is apparent; that he and the aesthetic movement introduced the word "dude" to the language is less well known.[30]

In Denver, Wilde told a reporter that "California is an Italy without its art. There are subjects for the artist, but it is universally true that the only scenery which inspires utterance is that which man feels himself the master of. The mountains of California are so gigantic that they

16. THE VASTNESS OF THE LANDSCAPE, AS SHOWN
HERE TOWERING OVER THE CAMPSITE, WAS A COMMON
THEME IN TEXT AND ILLUSTRATIONS.

Our camp in the Sweetwater Country. Arthur Pendarves
Vivian. *Wanderings in the Western Land* (1879). p. 301. Courtesy
University of Idaho Library.

are not favorable to art or poetry." He added,
"There are good poets in England but none in
Switzerland. There the mountains are too high.
Art cannot add to nature."[31] Here, and when
he described the Rockies as "perhaps the most
beautiful part of the West,"[32] Wilde paid one of
his few respectful tributes to the American landscape. Of the West, he said, "it all interests me
very much."[33]

Like many travellers, Wilde compared the
Rockies to the Alps; he described his trip to
"Colorado which is like the Tyrol a little, and
has great cañons of red sandstone, and pine trees,

and the tops of the mountains all snow-covered."
And, in the same letter, he noted the miners
looked "so picturesque in the dim light as they
swung the hammers and cleft the stone."[34] But
Switzerland's mountains he also called "big,"
"ugly," and "all black and white like an enormous photograph."[35]

A creature of gas-lit drawing rooms, Wilde
once quipped, "I detest nature where man has not
intervened with his artifice."[36] This is surprisingly close to the previous century's fashion for
landscape that was only viewed as picturesque
when it included a human-scaled object for comparison. This sensibility will be examined more
closely in the next chapter. On another occasion,
Wilde said, "I hate views – they are only made
for bad painters."[37] More appropriately, perhaps,
and less epigrammatically, Wilde also argued that
magnificence in nature could not be improved
by art.

Wilde appreciated the opportunities to be
found in the West. To one young admirer, James
E. Babb, following a lecture at a Midwestern

college, Wilde "said that if he were a young man in this country the West would have great charms for him." Ten years later, Babb, undoubtedly taking Wilde's advice, arrived in Lewiston, Idaho. He became a pillar of the local community and a lecturer at the University of Idaho's College of Law.[38]

After his jaunt into the mining country above Denver, Wilde, in his stage costume of knee-breeches, tried to persuade his eastern audiences that the western miner's boots and wide-brimmed hats were appropriate apparel for men. Even cartoonist Thomas Nast caricatured Wilde's endorsement of western wear in *Harper's Bazaar*.[39]

Back in London, Wilde continued his touring success by lecturing on America to the Britons. Witty and condescending, he described the tourists at Niagara as "trying to get up that feeling of sublimity which the guide books assured them they could do without extra charge." Of the western plains, he said they "conveyed the impression that nature had given up the job of decorating the country, so vast its size, in absolute despair."[40] In 1887, after a brief return to New York, he commented more approvingly of the American landscape and, especially, the prairie: "Better the Far West with its grizzly bears and its untamed cow-boys, its free open-air life and its free open-air manners, its boundless prairie, and its boundless mendacity."[41] The latter is undoubtedly a reference to the theatrical excesses of Buffalo Bill's Wild West Show, appearing in London at that time.

The crux of Wilde's aesthetic vision was that there was beauty in more things than just art; but he did not deny that there was much ugliness in the world. True to form, he thought beautiful scenery so commonplace as to be not worth mentioning. His job was to seek out beauty in the unlikeliest of places. Not for Oscar Wilde were the standard vistas, the picturesque landscapes, the set pieces of landscape art and reality. His epigrams against "Nature" include: "Nature is a foolish place to look for inspiration in, but a charming one in which to forget one ever had any."[42] And, "I am on bad terms with Nature: I see in her neither intellect nor passion – the only two things that make surfaces possible for me. I allude of course to what is termed Landscape."[43]

Yet he could write an evocative and descriptive paragraph, illuminating the landscape with his pen. From San Francisco, he wrote to his friend, actor Norman Forbes-Robertson, of his train trip:

I was four days in the train; at first grey, gaunt desolate plains, as colourless as waste land by the sea, with now and then scampering herds of bright red antelopes, and heavy shambling buffaloes, rather like [London theatre critic] Joe Knight in manner and appearance, and screaming vultures like gnats high up in the air, then up the Sierra Nevadas, the snow-capped mountains shining like shields of polished silver in that vault of blue flame we call the sky, and deep cañons full of pine trees.[44]

Wilde went on to literary success in London as a novelist, playwright, and epigrammatist, until he was publicly charged and convicted for homosexual behaviour. Upon his release from prison, he sailed to France, living under an assumed name. He died there penniless at the age of forty-six.

Standing Upon the Mountaintop

Although Henry M. Stanley became famous for his explorations and exploits on another continent, he managed to work in some adventures in the United States as well. Born out of wedlock in Wales in 1841 and neglected by his family, Stanley had a hard childhood. Jumping ship as a youth in New Orleans, he eventually served on both sides during the American Civil War. First, he fought with the rebels at Shiloh before being captured. Then, he briefly joined the Union army to escape the regimen of a prisoner of war camp. Later, he was with the U.S. Navy in its assault on Fort Fisher, North Carolina. Resuming his travels, Stanley went back to England, and then returned to the United States to California, with a stop in 1865 and 1866 to work briefly in

Colorado's Central City and nearby Black Hawk City. With another adventurer, he took a flatboat the six-hundred miles down the Platte to Omaha, suffered bizarre adventures in Turkey, and returned to the West as a journalist to follow the campaigns of Major General Winfield Scott Hancock against the Plains Indians.[45]

On his return to Colorado in 1867, Stanley's reports were submitted to both St. Louis and New York newspapers. His journalistic success led quickly to travels in Africa, and subsequent fame and notoriety. These western dispatches, somewhat revised, were published in 1895 as *My Early Travels and Adventures in America and Asia* after his fame had been well established. While landscape was not the principal topic of his reports, it managed to intrude itself, sometimes in a metaphorical manner:

I determined to devote an afternoon to a ramble over the mountains. I travelled a road gently ascending towards Nevada and Idaho Cities; I then walked a mile east of Missouri City; along the highest ridge, but continually ascending until I stood on the topmost point, I had been four hours walking, seeing nothing very remarkable; but the view now stretched before me amply compensated me for any trouble I had taken.[46]

This "ramble" led him to a mountain peak from which he could see the mountains to the west shrouded in the coming darkness, the range of mountains to the north and south, and the vast plains to the east.

Looking westward, I saw the sun gradually descend beyond the seemingly illimitable heights, each rough peak and mountain top clearly defined, while long dark shadows covered the eastern slopes. Away to the northward rose peak upon peak till lost in an infinity of snowy

whiteness, the whole view rendered beautifully distinct
and brilliant by the sun. Above all towered Long's Peak,
fully one hundred miles distant direct north, yet each
ravine, fissure, and crag seen distinctly. To the south-
ward lay Pike's Peak, surrounded by myriads of peaks
of lesser height, and covered with eternal snow. I was
standing almost equi-distant between the two highest
mountains, while an area of five hundred square miles
was spread out. A portion of Montana was, I believe,
visible; I caught a glimpse of future Wyoming; and my
eyes rested upon a corner of New Mexico.[47]

While "future" Wyoming and New Mexico
might have been seen from this vantage, it is
unlikely that Montana's corner was in sight.
With the clarity of mountain vision, and the
knowledge that construction was underway,
Stanley makes a bold prediction:

Standing upon the mountain top in the red evening
sunlight, which sheds a golden lustre upon earth and
sky, I predict, that this country will be acknowledged in
the coming future as no mean State. Time is flying, the

iron horse is upon the plain, impatient to rush through
the heart of the mountain towards the Pacific. Two years
hence the dwellers upon the Atlantic slopes will unite
hands with their brothers of the Pacific shores, and then
– and then will the desert rejoice, and the wilderness be
made glad.[48]

Again, like many travellers in the West, Stanley
was not hesitant to compare the Rockies with
the Alps. "All around us are lofty mountains
and forest solitude. I have seen grand Tauran
scenery, Alpine and Pyrenean mountains, about
which much has been said, but they are puny
in comparison with the grandeur of the Rocky
Mountains."[49] Stanley's recent biographers have
demonstrated that he was frequently misleading
in his writings about himself; it is not necessarily true that he was speaking from the personal
experience that he claimed. There is, for example, little evidence that he had actually visited
the Pyrenees or the Alps; while the documents of
his Turkish travels, where the Tauros Mountains
loom, are inconclusive.[50]

Of another "romantic place," he writes that it "equals in its wild solitude and loveliness any Alpine valley ever seen."[51] And of the mountains around Golden, Colorado, he wrote, "Crossing Clear Creek, we enter the most wonderful portion of America, the great mountains, by the 'Golden Gate,' their natural portal. The scenery is inexpressibly wild and majestic. On each side of the cañon rise dizzy heights, the slopes of which are covered by shrubs and plants, luxuriant creepers, where grape vines, wild raspberry and strawberry grow in profusion."[52]

Stanley was quite taken by the profusion of plant and animal life in the Colorado mountains, perhaps enough to overstate their quantity and quality. These little wilderness vignettes provide background and atmosphere to his more prosaic accounts of Indian "wars" and peace talks:

We have entered the heart of the mountains and are enclosed on all sides by threatening crags and lofty hills crowned by dark pineries, above which soar the ravens, their romantic "caw ca–aw" sounding shrill and clear in the rocky solitude around. Feathered songsters hop from bush to bush, and delight our ears with their cheering notes; strange insects go buzzing and humming gaily in the air. Beautifully minute, humble flowers of unknown name bloom sweetly and refreshingly under the shade of the birch, along the margin of the creek. Here we come to a large moss–covered boulder, which appears to invite the "weary toiler up the rugged steep" to a seat, while a sparkling streamlet issuing from underneath forms a slight cascade as it falls over a bed of quartz of snowy whiteness. We permit our delighted eyes to wander over a nature fresh in its vernal bloom, and to admire its richness, to which the streaming sunshine gives a varying and animated complexion.[53]

Stanley didn't stay long in the West; his restlessness was ensured by his unsettled childhood. By December 1867, he quit his arrangement with the St. Louis newspaper and offered to cover African campaigns for James Gordon Bennett Jr.'s *New York Tribune*. Among the other reporters covering the colonial wars in Africa in the early 1870s was Windham Thomas Wyndham-

Quin, later the Earl of Dunraven, who was to purchase a Rocky Mountain empire in Estes Park above Denver.[54] Although the same age, Stanley and Lord Dunraven came from widely divergent and frequently antagonistic backgrounds. Stanley's aggressive defensiveness about his low status caused problems both with the British officers and the other members of the press corps during his early days in Africa.[55] Accordingly, it is unlikely that Lord Dunraven's interest in the American West derived from Stanley's experiences.

Stanley's greatest accomplishment in Africa, of course, was his successful search in 1871 for the missionary explorer Dr. David Livingstone, a task he accomplished just in advance of the expedition sent out by the Royal Geographical Society. Stanley's next assignment was to report on General Garnet Wolseley's campaign against the Ashanti in West Africa. Wolseley and Stanley grew to admire each other's military qualities after a somewhat rocky start. The general did not like journalists, but found Stanley's bravery during battle – for instance, a stead-fast Stanley kept firing away in the face of the enemy, a contradiction of the normal role of a military correspondent – admirable indeed.[56] Wolseley had gained some fame as the youthful commander of the British effort to put out the flames of Canada's Red River Rebellion. His intelligence officer during that earlier campaign was the same William F. Butler whose winter journey across the northern Rockies originated from the Geographical Society's decision to choose the navy rather than the army to staff the Livingstone rescue expedition. Still, there is no record that Wolseley and Stanley were close enough to exchange tales about experiences in the North American West.

Bolder and Keener Contours

Another British traveller who spent more than a few weeks in the United States was poet James Thomson. Born of poor parents in 1834, Thomson became known both as a contributor to the free-thought, secularist, and atheistic movement and as a poet of depression and what is today called *anomie*, or disorientation. His poetic stance seems to have greatly overtaken his personal attributes, compounded perhaps by his increasing alcoholism, and leading to his early death in 1882. In person, he was a charming and entertaining companion; however, these qualities were not enough to sustain him above poverty level.[57]

Although he seldom strayed far from the occupation of writer, he more than once attempted a business career. As a consequence, in 1872 he found himself at Central City, Colorado, near Denver, as the secretary of the Champion Gold and Silver Mines Company. The company directors had sent him to the West to oversee their diminishing investment in the mine. His activities on behalf of the company, faithfully recorded in a memorandum book, took up so much of his time that he wrote no poetry during his stay.[58] Yet, his time in Colorado was considered by many of his friends and biographers to be among "his pleasantest and most enjoyable experiences."[59] As proof, one reporter noted that,

"There is no evidence in [his] diary to indicate even a single period of intemperance."[60]

The writing Thomson did in Colorado was primarily of a business nature, except for his diary entries. The diary, now in the Bodleian Library, Oxford, shows Thomson adjusting to the magnitude of the western landscape. At first, his descriptions were straightforward with little in the way of interpretation. For instance, on May 23, soon after his arrival, he wrote:

Nearer Central all covered with large fir cones tho' scarcely a fir tree is now left. Plenty of snow on the hills – Near Central skinned of their timber and torn & scarred with mining, and rounded in low curves, the hills look new. Yet here and there behind are glimpses bolder & keener contours dark with fir. Coming back this morning I saw some of this kind, through the floating film of blue grey smoke, & at the utmost horizon the strip of blue beneath level white cloud could not be distinguished from a sea.[61]

Over time, however, the landscape took on a larger impact. Idaho Springs, after a June rain, was "about as beautiful a place as I ever saw."[62] The transforming quality of nature in its mountain glory also had an effect:

The hills and mountains never the same for five minutes together in form, colour or expression. The shadows shifting, the forms varying, the lights changing, the colours running through a hundred different shades. Enjoyed myself very much, and thought with a certain vigour as I used to think.[63]

In his letters from Colorado, Thomson took the time to make more than brief notes. To his pre-Raphaelite friend William M. Rossetti, he wrote:

These foothills are distributed remarkably amongst the snowy ranges of the mountains, curtain beyond curtain, fold within fold, twisting and heaving inextricably. Those immediately around [Central City] are of flat tame curves, as if crouching to their abject mercenary doom; but beyond there are keen crests and daring serrated contours, green with firs and cottonwood-aspens

or nobly dark with pines; and one massy range ends in a promontory whose scarped precipitous upper flank gleams grand and savage in its stony nakedness, like the gleaming of set white teeth in some swart Titanic barbarian.[64]

The narrow mountain valleys of the east slope of the Colorado Rockies are perfectly captured here in somewhat effusive prose. He continued his exposition, looking out over the landscape, attempting to describe it to his friend back in England:

From these higher hills one gets magnificent views; vast billowy land seas, with dense woods and deep ravines and exquisite emerald dells, whereon and wherever sleep and sweep immense shadows, and of all shades even at noonday, from bright green to solid black; beyond, a crescent of the mountains, some with broad fields or deep furrows of snow, some sheathed wholly with this white splendour; eastward toward the plains, what the keenest eye cannot distinguish from a distant sea-line, faint or dark blue, level to the horizon, with pale streaks like

Mountains So Sublime

the shadows of clouds and long shoals and the haze of evaporation.[65]

If Thomson refrained from purely literary writing in Colorado, can it be said that his experiences influenced his later work? The only directly related prose piece is the satirical "Religion in the Rocky Mountains," part of which was published in the *National Reformer* after his return to London. Although it contains little related to landscape, it is well worth reading for its presentation of "the insincerities of good churchmen in the practice of everyday life," as presented in "striking illustrations drawn from typical Western life."[66] Of his poetry, there are descriptive passages on landscape that appear in his major work, "City of Dreadful Night," and in the poem "Insomnia" that might be based on his Colorado experiences.[67] A more resonant and intriguing influence was made on the younger author, Rudyard Kipling. It has been stated that when Kipling had one of his frequent bouts of insomnia, he would wander about, contemplating the "City of Dreadful Night," which he had first read in school. In addition, Kipling went on to borrow the title for one of his own works.[68]

The "City of Dreadful Night" is not particularly rural in nature; it is a city-dweller's nightmare with its depressing images of grey buildings and impenetrable darkness. It can easily be attributed specifically to London, where Thomson spent most of his life. Although he began writing it in early 1872, "City of Dreadful Night" was not completed until his return from Colorado.[69] However, more than one observer believes the following lines were drawn from Thomson's experience in the West:

A trackless wilderness rolls north and west,
Savannahs, savage woods, enormous mountains,
Bleak uplands, black ravines with torrent fountains....[70]

The latter seems to have been taken directly from the "deep ravines [of] solid black" he described in his letter to Rossetti. Also possibly derived from his Colorado experiences is:

The hillock burning with brazen glare;
Those myriad dusky flames with points a-glow....[71]

It has been suggested that the "brazen hillock" was based on "the licking flames of a burning mine dump," although there is no indication in Thomson's diary that he ever saw such a sight.[72]

It would be as easy to say that the later expression, "Athwart the mountains and immense wild tracts," is also a direct reflection of Colorado.[73] On the other hand, a brief mention of "opium visions" could, of course, relate either to Chinese people in Central City (which he mentioned in a letter to W. M. Rossetti)[74] or to the Chinese community in Limehouse, East London.

A more obvious example of western imagery, a saloon scene, could also be drawn from London's underworld as well as Colorado's; Thomson was undoubtedly familiar with both:

From drinking fiery poison in a den
Crowded with tawdry girls and squalid men,
Who hoarsely laugh and curse and brawl and fight:
I wake from daydreams to this real night.[75]

It is not "City of Dreadful Night" that carries the most extensive description of western landscape; it is the lesser, but still powerful, poem entitled "Insomnia." The images of night, sleep, waking, and despair are all there as they were in "City of Dreadful Night," but in addition, there are the following striking stanzas:

And saw the night before me an immense
Black waste of ridge-walls, hour by hour apart,
Dividing deep ravines: from ridge to ridge
Sleep's flying hour was an aërial bridge;
But I, whose hours stood fast,
Must climb down painfully each steep side hither,
And climb more painfully each steep side thither,
And so make one hour's span for years of travail last.

Thus I went down into that first ravine,
Wearily, slowly, blindly, and alone,
Staggering, stumbling, sinking depths unseen,
Shaken and bruised and gashed by stub and stone;
And at the bottom paven with slipperiness,
A torrent-brook rushed headlong with such stress
Against my feeble limbs,

Such fury of wave and foam and icy bleakness
Buffeting insupportably my weakness
That when I would recall, dazed memory swirls and
*   swims.*[76]

Yet "Insomnia's" specific characterization of the difficulties of mountain travel was apparently written almost a decade after Thomson left Central City, and just before his early death from alcoholism in 1882. Thomson enjoyed his eight months in Colorado, and at one point considered making his stay permanent.[77] As it was, he returned to England without any prospects, and then he tried being a journalist in Spain, a clerk in London, and, ultimately, a writer for a tobacconist's propaganda magazine. He returned, one biographer wrote, "a mature pessimist and a confident atheist."[78]

Thomson, like Kipling, Stevenson, Wilde, and Stanley, found the North American western landscape both a receptacle for his own stereotypes and a source of overwhelming beauty and grandeur. The western wilderness was not a source of personal redemption, nor did it, by itself, significantly change the course of each man's literary development. Yet each was affected, and the impact of their travels can be measured in their writings. Each writer was also moved to write about what he had seen. Among them, Oscar Wilde's apt description to Forbes-Robertson of the Sierras as "the snow-capped mountains shining like shields of polished silver in that vault of blue flame we call the sky" captures perfectly the stunning quality of the western landscape.

The Post-Picturesque Landscape

4

After 70 miles the country became picturesque again in the Thompson valley, the river in the valley below of the most brilliant green under a sky of deep blue.[1]

While the western landscape was fresh and diverse to these new viewers, the British travellers' aesthetic sensibilities had a much longer history. The representation, in words, of a visual scene such as a landscape has tasked poets and other authors from the early days of written language. Much of the ability to communicate verbally in a comprehensible fashion results from a sharing of terms and expectations between the author and the audience. For the British traveller of the late nineteenth century, this common vocabulary tended to be derived from what one scholar has labelled three possible world views: "the fashionable, the informative and the utilitarian."[2]

This categorization provides a framework for the discussion of textual landscape descriptions. However, it is an artificial construct, and does not entirely corral any particular author's choice of words in the context of the western landscape. It has been suggested that adopting one or more of these conventional "world views" meant that the travel writer would actually fail to accurately describe the specific landscape, because the mode of viewing filtered the scenery in such a way that the writer quite literally could not *see* it. That is to say that the conventions of description served less as descriptive tools than as blinders; instead of revealing the landscape, they concealed it behind "externally imposed presumptions."[3] Still, this may overstate the case. Sharing a common vocabulary tends to increase communication; that today's readers do not quite share the same vocabulary of nineteenth century British travel writers does not mean they were blind to the landscape. As one historian put it:

An explanation or description of the landscape and living conditions for people who have not seen them for themselves was made more meaningful by the use of analogies, comparisons, and similes with which not only the writer but also the reader was familiar. Obviously, what might have seemed tedious country to the tourist could convey important detail to the hunter or hint of greater potential to the farmer.[4]

Working backwards through the three world views, we find that the "utilitarian" mode considered landscape of no account unless put to profit for man. This schema is drawn from the world of capitalism and business, with a passing reference to the Bible, in which mankind is granted dominion over the earth. In this mode, description concentrated on those scenes that favoured farming, ranching, or mining. Scenery for the sake of scenery is either ignored or treated as an inducement to emigrants. Wilderness, unsuitable for cultivation or development, was described in disparaging terms. The "taming" of the landscape's wilderness is the dominant concept. British travellers were nearly unanimous in rejecting this utilitarian philosophy. "Man's exigencies," in Colon South's phrase, were often condemned.[5] Given the economic basis for many of the traveller's journeys, this is something of a surprise. It was certainly contrary to the point of view expressed by the locals, mostly farmers, ranchers, or miners.

The "informative" mode was favoured by explorers, engineers, geologists, and naturalists. The terminology is dryly descriptive, suitable for government reports. The world view that fostered this mode of description was drawn from the scientific method. For instance, many of the reports on British Columbia to the Royal Geographical Society in the 1860s concentrated on soils, rocks, and formations, but seldom contained any reference to the magnificence of the scenery. Yet not all of those who adopted this mode were necessarily scientists or persons with scientific training. For example, one scholar has noted instances of travellers adopting a debased version of the "informative" mode in their attempts to describe the indescribable wonders of the American West. Running out of descriptive terms, they would fall back to more objective-seeming language.[6] Lord Dunraven, on the other hand, showed his awareness of this tendency. Of his trip to Yellowstone Park, he wrote, "I did not undertake the expedition in the cause of Science. I do not pretend to anything but a very slight acquaintance with natural history, geology, and mineralogy. I had no instruments for taking measurements, nor the time, knowledge, and skill necessary to make advantageous use of them."[7]

The literary or "fashionable" mode was the one shared by most of the British travellers in the American West. Its roots were derived from the fruitful collision between the efforts of eighteenth century English aestheticians and French *philosophes*. Among its progenitors was William Gilpin, whose influence was as broad in his day, and as similar in its effect, as Walt Disney's fictional landcapes have been in recent years.[8] By bringing nature itself, instead of a painting of nature, into the aesthetic realm, his books of packaged picturesque tours created an artificial reality that encouraged sophisticated city dwellers to seek beauty in the outdoors. He did this by declaring certain views to be "picturesque" – that is to say, like a picture or painting. He shaped these picturesque views by identifying the exact point, known as the viewpoint, at which the Romantic tourist should stand. His books of picturesque tours marked these viewpoints in much the same way as do coin-operated telescopes at tourist viewpoints or the well-marked highway pull-offs. And, like the railings put up at the viewpoints, Gilpin's pre-packaged views protected the tourist from raw nature while allowing visual access.[9]

From the Picturesque to the Sublime

This picturesque view drew upon the conventions of landscape painting; a view was considered to be picturesque if it had a foreground, middle ground, and background, along with strong compositional elements, and, also, an "atmosphere." A greatly simplified example would be the mystery and sense of foreboding attached to a darkened landscape. In addition, a picturesque scene often contained what was called an "association." This was a narrative element that enhanced the scene by relating it to a stirring event, a major work of art, or a moral literary scene. It was this latter characteristic that made it so difficult for scenes in North America to be appreciated as picturesque, for they lacked the crumbling castles or churches that so often provided the "association" in European scenes. The rawness, wildness, and unfinished state of American scenery also detracted from its picturesque qualities.

Yet, if the Rocky Mountains could not be beautiful and attractive in the same way as the other picturesque tourist attractions throughout the world, they could be sublime. Like the picturesque, the expression of sublimity was linked to an emotional construct in the viewer's mind. A sublime view made one feel awe, wonder, and perhaps fear; without, of course, being physically threatening. The concept of the sublime was given widespread credibility by Edmund Burke's influential *A Philosophical Enquiry into the Origin of Our Ideas of the Sublime and Beautiful* (1756).[10] By 1825, Niagara Falls was accorded that label and became a tourist destination.[11] Soon afterward, the visual wealth of the Rocky Mountains was granted the same honour; these too were huge, awe-inspiring, grand, wild, and rugged. The Rockies also demonstrated "Nature's" majesty

and thus assumed aspects of the divinity. They were not, as a whole, considered picturesque, but they certainly were sublime.

As concepts, "sublime" and "picturesque" were not static elements. They grew and developed as part of the Romantic Revolution of the eighteenth century, and became entrenched and debased during the nineteenth century. Late in the eighteenth century, explorers on the Northwest Coast described the southern shores in picturesque terms, "pleasant and delightful," while the northern portion was "gloomy but sublime."[12] By 1809, poet William Combe and artist Thomas Rowlandson could satirize Gilpin and the picturesque notion in their popular and humorous "Dr. Syntax in Search of the Picturesque."[13] Syntax's eventful travels, which unfold in Combe's couplets and Rowlandson's plates, sprang from the learned Doctor's impulse to become a travel writer:

I'll prose it here, I'll verse it there,
And picturesque it ev'ry where.[14]

In the middle of the nineteenth century, writing about the Rocky Mountains, the whole satire was turned around again by travel author Maurice O'Connor Morris. He noted, "The Doctor Syntax school can here find the beautiful and picturesque in the amplest and wildest profusion; while the lover of the grand and majestic in nature, can here see his wildest dream realized."[15]

In fact, during the early part of the nineteenth century, the descriptive vocabulary of the Romantics spread downward through the culture, and began to merge into generalized sentiments of approbation.[16] If it was pretty, it was "picturesque;" if it was strange or ugly, yet of interest, it became "sublime." Examples range from the general statement that "large pine trees are growing picturesquely here and there,"[17] to one rough mountain landscape in another author's text which seemed "as if God's wrath had rested longer on this sublime chaos than on most other spots."[18]

Niagara Falls, so awesome as to attract tourists from all over the globe, "was a great stimulant to the Romantic imagination; it provided an example of divine sublimity found elsewhere only in the sea."[19] Yet by the third quarter of the nineteenth century, Niagara's majestic sublimity was no match for the American commercialism noticed by British travellers, "where advertisements of wonderful oils and successful pills are painted on the face of the splendid cliffs and rocks."[20] This was true of the Rockies as well:

Nothing grates on the nerves of the spectator of this grand scenery but the placards or painted advertisements stuck on every commanding peak, slab, or table rock. Messrs. Vandal and Shameless of Denver, are to be read everywhere on the face of nature forty miles to the mountains; and it takes several days to view their defacements of America's grandest scenery with calm contempt, a far more active feeling of disgust being at first awakened.[21]

While Americans' all-conquering passion for money-grubbing may have overwhelmed their appreciation of the sublime and the picturesque, British travellers continued to use these terms in their descriptions of the West. They were, however, no more consistent in their use than any other tourists. Attempts to move away from "aesthetic" descriptions of the landscape towards more informational or utilitarian modes were not wholly successful. Potential emigrants, settlers, and financiers wanted more data about soils, crops, and weather than touristy expressions of awe and wonder. But even the scientific explorers fell back on the picturesque as a mode of description. This was partly based on a realization that the emigrants and other consumers of this data were motivated as much by visions as by facts, and in part owing to an inability to avoid the developed vocabulary that permitted the description of an awesome and magnificent landscape.[22]

A naturalist member of a boundary survey expedition to the Pacific Northwest might be expected to discuss the breeding habits of ducks, beaver dens, or the migrations of salmon in scientific or informational terms. John Keast Lord, of the 1860s British Boundary Commission, went beyond the "informative" mode in his popular account, *The Naturalist in Vancouver Island and British Columbia,* to include a great deal of literary expressiveness as well. His description of Lower Klamath Lake in Oregon is an extensive mix of scientific and aesthetic concerns. Even as he provided the Latin names, noted the many different kinds of ducks, and indicated the precise colour of pelican legs and pouches; the beauty of the scenery (he calls it "picturesque"), stopped him in his tracks. The result is a delightful hybrid, a lyrical blend of the scientific and the Romantic:

Where could one find a more enjoyable sight, whether viewed with the eye of a naturalist or lover of the picturesque? Before me is the reedy swamp, with its open patches of water, glittering like mirrors in the bright sunlight, rippled in all directions by busy beavers: some making a hasty retreat to their castles, others swimming craftily along, crawl on to the domes and peep at the intruder. Dozing on the sandbanks round the margin of the pools, or paddling with 'oary feet' on the smooth water, are numbers of snowy pelicans: the bright orange encircling the eyes, and colouring the pouch, legs, and feet, looks like flame, contrasted with the white feathers, so intensified is the color by the brilliancy of the sun-rays. Pintails, shovelers, stockducks, the exquisitely coloured cinnamon teal, the noisy bald-pate, and a host of others, are either floating on the water or circling round in pairs, quacking angry remonstrances at such an unjustifiable prying into their nuptial haunts. Overhead, vieing with the swallows in rapidity and grace of flight, countless Terns (Sterna Foster) whir in mazy circles: their black heads, grey and white liveries, and orange-yellow beaks, show to great advantage against the sombre green of the swallows, amid which they wing their way. Behind me, and far to the right, the Sis-ky-oue Mountains, in many a rugged peak, bound the sky-line, their slopes descending in an unbroken surface of pine-trees to the grassy flats at their

base. To my left, the river that feeds this rushy lake winds through the green expanse, like a line of twisted silver, far as the eye can scan its course; along its bank my string of mules, in dingy file, pace slowly on: the tinkle of the bell-horse, but faintly audible, bids me hasten after them, and leave a scene the like of which I shall never perhaps gaze on again.[23]

Another British traveller, novelist George A. Lawrence, makes a specific comparison between "scientific" and "aesthetic" descriptions: "An artist's eye might find attractions here, even at this dreary season; though the sternness of the huge cliff-walls on either hand is enhanced rather than softened by the fringes of stunted pines, clinging and climbing where-ever they can find foot-hold; and there are studies for the geologist, in the rapid and abrupt changes of 'formations' wherever the rocks stand out bare."[24] The result, except for the "stunted pines," is a description that does not describe.

S. N. Townshend, whose articles on Colorado were published between 1876 and 1878 in the

English magazine *The Field*, frequently described
the landscape in aesthetic terms. In one passage,
about Manitou Park, the drive in is "as lovely
and romantic as the mind can imagine." Without
using the term "picturesque," Townshend reports
"gorgeous mountain passes; the golden sunshine
on the dazzling snow; vast pines towering over
roaring, babbling, singing brooks; red and purple
precipices, so high as to shut out the sun from
their gloomy but grand cañons even at eleven
o'clock in the day; occasionally a broad open
park, with dry gravelly soil and golden grass."
Here, he ranges over the landscape from the
far-distant peaks, through the middle ground
of pines, brooks, and precipices, to the "golden
grass" just before him. At the end of the passage,
shifting towards the sublimity of the scene, he
proclaims that, "a sense of immensity and overwhelming force takes precedence of the mere
idea of beauty in such a place as this."[25]

Elsewhere, Townshend finds that "a more
lovely and picturesque scene could not have met
my eye." Here, his eye traverses the landscape in
the reverse direction, from near to far; first, the
"villa" where he lodged, next, the "mammoth
red sandstone rocks" in the middle ground, and
finally, the far distant "foot hills of the immor-
tal Rockies." One element of the picturesque
not usually found in the American West was
the romantic ruin. But the natural wonders of
the landscape more than made up for the lack.
Townshend found the red sandstone rocks to be
"of remarkable and fantastic forms, of which one
was twice as high as the house – faces with eyes
only, faces with nothing but noses, points like an
alligator's mouth, flat rocks, round rocks, spires,
and boulders, all brilliant red against a pure
white background."[26]

Townshend also discerned architectural features in the geology; these added to the landscape's picturesque qualities: "The extraordinary perpendicular crests of the hills in the isolated valleys are quite palatial; and as dusk draws on, anyone not having seen the country by daylight would imagine that the haughty Spanish owners of the district in the 16th century had permanently impressed their lordly style of architecture on the territory. This is by far the most picturesque in the west."[27] The "palatial" rockeries, of course, added to the picturesqueness by giving it a conjectured European origin.

The West is full of "fantastic" rocks, either in shape, or in colour, or both. And, many were characterized as architectural ruins, thus passing to them the associations from European landscape that were considered sorely lacking in the Americas. To W. A. Baillie-Grohman, the rocks seemed like "the battlemented walls of a Norman keep, sorely battered by time," or like a "bizarre array of pinnacles, turrets, and bold fantastic carvings imitating architectural forms, and suggesting rude but weird statuary."[28] To Isabella Bird they were like "the similitude of stately fortresses, not the gray castellated towers of feudal Europe, but gay, massive, Saracenic architecture, the out-growth of the solid rock."[29]

Not all formations were characterized as European architectural ruins. Some, at least, were, according to B.C. miner R. B. Johnson, "in the shapes of castles, needle-points, men's faces, and every other curious conceivable thing, and in a brilliant sunrise, or a glowing sunset, the scene was utterly beyond words to describe, or the artist's pencil to paint, in its immeasurable grandeur."[30]

In Europe, the term "picturesque" was usually applied to the natural landscape, a river valley or a lake, perhaps with a ruined castle or abbey. Isabella Bird found the picturesque in a Colorado mining town. "The area on which it is possible to build [in Georgetown] is so circumscribed and steep, and the unpainted gable-ended houses are so perched here and there, and the water rushes so impetuously among them, that it reminded me slightly of a Swiss town. All the smaller houses are shored up with young pines on one side, to prevent them from being blown away by the fierce gusts which sweep the canyon. It is the only town I have seen in America to which the epithet picturesque could be applied."[31] Yet even this characterization of the picturesque required a European element to make it complete.

The contrasting technique is to focus on what is not picturesque. Of the towns nestled in Colorado's Front Range, Maurice O'Connor Morris thought they "would be very picturesque were it not for the bareness of the surrounding mountains, which have been denuded of their shade and ornament; but the views in the neighborhood are fine, though monotonous."[32] Similarly, Vicar Zincke found the Front Range deficient in picturesqueness. "From the picturesque point of view, the defect of the mountains is that they keep too much to the straight line."[33] In general agreement was W. A. Baillie-Grohman, who noted:

In viewing spacious panoramic landscape in America, one generally finds that the eye rarely encounters specific points about it that leave a lasting impression. When on some future occasion one endeavors to reconstruct the picture, it is far more puzzling than had it been European Alpine scenery. The picturesque details about the latter, far more numerous and far more varied, can somehow, much more easily be remembered.[34]

The clue to his difficulty perhaps is in his use of the phrase "spacious panoramic landscape." The vastness of the American West was so often overwhelming that it was difficult to find details to hang onto. In fact, to most, the Rockies were less picturesque than they were sublime. "The Rockies, when once you devote yourself entirely to seeing them, put shooting aside, and go direct from one point of grand scenery to another, must certainly etherialise the most unpoetic mind," wrote S. N. Townshend, drawing upon the relationship between the sublime and the divine in nature.[35]

What the Rocky Mountain West lacked in picturesqueness, it more than made up for in sublimity, the awesome power of nature that speaks of divinity; God's works made manifest on the landscape. Picturesque scenes were frequently small, human-sized, or at least scaled to humans. They had comprehensible elements, such as structures, rock formations, animals, or people. The beauties that were sublime, however, were overwhelming; they were wild and they were vast. They connected with the infinite. And it was in the sublimity of their landscapes that Americans, such failures at the picturesque, were finally able to lord it over the Europeans.[36]

Naturalist John Keast Lord was very explicit about the feelings of sublimity he found in Canada's Rocky Mountain West. "There was a wild grandeur about the scene, that awoke feelings of awe rather than admiration; everywhere vast piles of craggy mountains, clad from the snow-line to the sea with dense pine-forests; not an open grassy spot, or even a naked mass of rock, peeped out to break the fearful monotony of these interminable hills."[37]

In the interior of British Columbia, the scene was no less sublime for the presence of a Native campsite, and he chose not to call it picturesque, although he described it in decidedly picturesque terms:

Before me, stretching away for about three miles, is an open grassy prairie, one side of which is bounded by the Chilukweyuk river, the other by the Fraser. At the junction of the two streams, at an angle of the prairie, stands an Indian village: the rude-plank sheds and rush-lodges; the white smoke, curling gracefully up through the still atmosphere from many lodge-fires; the dusky forms of the savages, as they loll or stroll in the fitful night, give life and character to a scene indescribably lovely.

The Indian summer is drawing to a close; the maple, the cottonwood, and the hawthorn, fringing the winding waterways, like silver cords intersecting the prairie, have assumed their autumn tints, and, clad in browns and yellows, stand out in brilliant contrast to the green of the pine-forest. The prairie looks bright and lovely; the grass, as yet untouched by the frost-fairy's fingers, waves lazily; wild flowers, of varied tints, peep out from their hiding-places, enjoying to the last the lingering summer.

I had been for some time sitting on a log, admiring the sublime beauty of the scene, spread out before me like a gorgeous picture; the sun was fast receding behind the hilltops, the lengthening shadows were fading and

Mountains So Sublime

growing dimly indistinct, the birds had settled down to sleep, and the busy hum of insect life was hushed.[38]

In the effort to transmit in words the effect of the western landscape, many authors made use of an aesthetic yardstick, what might be called a "sublimity scale," that made possible direct comparisons between the Rockies and the European Alps. The Rockies were more often compared to the Alps, and Colorado to Switzerland, than to any other region. W. A. Baillie-Grohman, for example, ranked the Rockies more sublime than the Alps on his sublimity scale:

Many of the Colorado mountains are called the Matterhorns of America — with about as much justification as the more diminutive Ben Nevis, or Snowden, merits that name. With the Teton it is, however, different; for it makes, so far as I know, the only and very brilliant exception to the unusual dome-like formation of the Rockies. In shape it is very like the Swiss masterpeak; but inasmuch as the Western rival rises in one majestic sweep of 7000 feet from this natural park, to an altitude all but the same (13,800 feet), I would, in this *instance, in point of sublimity give the palm to the New World.*[39]

A contrary view was expressed by A. B. Legard, who admitted he had only seen the Alps in photographs. Even so, he conjectured, "I should say it would puzzle the cleverest artist to find scenes in the Rocky Mountains equal to those which I have seen of the Alps."[40] Those travellers who were insulated from actual contact with the mountains by their railroad parlour cars were most likely to find the Rockies lacking in sublimity. But for those who got in among the mountains, as did John Keast Lord, W. A. Baillie-Grohman, and Richard Burton, the experience was quite different. Naturalist Lord and hunter Baillie-Grohman both traversed much of their respective routes on horseback. Burton, crossing into Utah by stagecoach, noted that:

The sublime and the beautiful were in present contrast. Switzerland and Italy lay side by side. The magnificent scenery of the past mountains and ravines still floated before the retina, as emerging from the gloomy depths of

20. THE RUGGED WESTERN LANDSCAPE WAS
PHOTOGRAPHED IN AN EFFORT TO CONVEY ITS
ENORMITY AND SCALE.

The arid interior uplands of B.C. William A. Baillie-
Grohman. *Fifteen Years' Sport and Life in the Hunting Grounds
of Western America and British Columbia* (1900). opp. p. 41.
Courtesy University of Idaho Library.

*the Golden Pass – the mouth of Emigration Kanyon is
more poetically so called – we came suddenly in view of
the Holy Valley of the West.*[41]

Scientific description was often abandoned
to aesthetics in describing the wonders of the
Rocky Mountain West. John Keast Lord, as a
naturalist, used precise scientific terms in his
description of the Lower Palouse Falls just above
the Snake River Canyon. But objective scientific
description quickly gave way in the face of the
grandness and sublimity of the scenery:

*I have never seen a more grand or stranger-looking
waterfall than this of the Lower pelouse. The trail I
follow is about a quarter of a mile from the river, winding in tortuous course between immense fragments of
rock, that completely hide the country to my left; ahead,
a line of splintered peaks denotes the course of the river
cañon; behind, I gaze back upon the Snake river, and
the stupendous cliffs beetling over its frothy water; to my
right, a grassy slope, smooth and green as a well-kept
lawn, extends for miles, until lost in the distant haze.
A heavy thundering sound directs me to the cataract,
which is at present hidden. I walk down the slope, and
unexpectantly reach the edge of a narrow channel, about
thirty feet in width and three hundred in depth.*

*Not a hundred yards from where I stand, the entire
river plunges over a vertical face of smooth rocks; down
it surges a depth of 300 feet, and possibly more, into the
narrow channel into which I am looking. The singular-
ity of this fall consists in the extremely narrow channel of
basaltic rock through which the entire river is obliged to
make its way before it dashes down this wondrous cliff.
The river, at least a hundred feet wide on the plain, is
narrowed to about thirty at the place where it falls over*

the rocks; hence the water leaps, if I may so express it, some distance from the rock on emerging from this natural launder, and falls vertically into the black chasm with a deafening roar like perpetual thunder.

The sun shining brightly lights up the gloomy chasm, and gives the foaming current a brilliancy unlike anything I have ever seen – an effect heightened and intensified by contrast. I may aptly liken it, without any attempt at word-painting, to a stream of liquid silver flowing through a channel of jet. As the rays of light mingle with the spray, that hangs like a dense fog round the watery column, their prismatic colours are reflected from myriads of tiny water-drops, making fairy rainbows, that dance in mazy clusters from the base to the summit of the fall. Not a tree or shrub is anywhere visible, nothing but rock and water – a scene matchless in its immensity. I am not so much charmed with the beauty of this wild landscape, as awed and (if I may so express it) absorbed and lost in its wonder; its sublime grandeur impresses me with a feeling that it is something more than earthly.[42]

Artist Paul Kane thought the entrance to the falls was "one of the boldest and most sublime passes the eye ever beheld."[43] He went on to quickly sketch both the upper and lower falls and later turned them into a series of several oil paintings.[44]

Baillie-Grohman, overlooking Jackson Hole in Wyoming, stopped his horse to sketch the scene, using his saddle as an easel. The Snake River, lined with cottonwood trees and curving through a green park-like landscape, surrounded by craggy mountains, led him to exclaim: "It was the most sublime scenery I have ever seen."[45] But in his description, which focused on the visual sequence from the foreground to the background and not on the scene's grandeur, he might as well have called it picturesque. Ever the sportsman, he found huntable game to add to the picturesque quality of a scene. "One lake you will see with a great Wapiti stag or quaintly uncouth Moose standing knee-deep in the water, or the presence of beaver will give it the peculiar charm of inhabitedness; while the next one, just as picturesquely situated, will have about it a lifeless, desolate air, that detracts from its idyllic loveliness."[46]

For most of those, American or English, writing about the Rocky Mountain West in the latter half of the nineteenth century, the sublime and picturesque were just terms of approval. One scholar noted this characteristic in Francis Parkman's personal journal of his western experiences.[47] The descriptive terms "sublime," referring to the awesome, and "picturesque," denoting a narrative painting-like quality, were established nearly a century and a half before the West became a visual destination. Accordingly, these definitions changed and, to some extent, merged. There are countless examples of this aesthetic confusion among the authors studied here. Richard Burton, for instance, described the "sublimity" of Echo Canyon's "broken and jagged peaks ... and scattered rocks" and proceeds to "remark the wonderful picturesqueness of a scene – of a nature which in parts seemed lately to have undergone some grand catastrophe."[48]

It was not uncommon for the writer to merely proclaim the "picturesqueness" of the scenery without trying to describe it. For instance, John Bodley, writing in his diary during his 1888 Canadian Pacific crossing of the Rockies, straightforwardly asserts that, "Glacier House is a picturesque chalet in a nook of the Selkirks just below the great glacier."[49] No description was given, just the bald statement that the otherwise unreproduced picturesque element makes it worthy of notice.

The Observer as Artist

The change in terminology corresponded to some degree to the changing conceptions of landscape painting. Today, it is seldom understood the extent to which artistic training was commonplace among the educated of the nineteenth century. Until photography became a consumer activity in the 1890s, it was not unusual for diaries and letters to be embellished with small descriptive drawings. At times, these were published not as professional artworks, but as illustrations of the text. Arthur Pendarves Vivian's *Wanderings in the Western Land* (1879) included illustrations drawn both by himself and by the prominent American landscape painter,

Albert Bierstadt. John Turner-Turner's accounts of hunting in America, *Three Years' Hunting and Trapping in America and the Great North-West* (1888) are illustrated, probably from his own or his wife's sketches, by illustrator Constance Hoare. The coloured lithographs in Frank Marryat's *Mountains and Molehills* (1855) were based on his drawings of the California gold rush. In much the same fashion, portrait painter Frederick Piercy's 1853 account of his travels with a Mormon wagon train includes "steel engravings and woodcuts from [his] sketches."[50] Burton's *City of the Saints* (1862) and Isabella Bird's *A Lady's Life in the Rocky Mountains* (1879) also include numerous illustrations. In her later travels, Bird became an avid photographer.

Sir Charles Dilke's *Greater Britain; A Record of Travel in English-Speaking Countries, during 1866–7* (1868) includes both maps and illustrations, as does Baillie-Grohman's *Camps in the Rockies. Being a Narrative of Life on the Frontier, and Sport in the Rocky Mountains, with an Account of the Cattle Ranches of the West* (1882). His later *Fifteen Years' Sport and Life in the Hunting Grounds of Western America and British Columbia* (1900) is illustrated by photographs. *The Great Divide: Travels in the Upper Yellowstone in the Summer of 1874* (1876) by Lord Dunraven includes illustrations by the English painter and illustrator Valentine W. Bromley. The Reverend George M. Grant's *Ocean to Ocean* (1873) is also illustrated. Of the identified illustrators, perhaps only Bierstadt and Bromley achieved major recognition for their art; few professionals, it is said, were attracted to the North American landscape.[51]

But many of those listed above were themselves artists, even if only amateurs. Railroad engineer Sir Sandford Fleming made sketches throughout his trans-Canada expedition, less for art perhaps than to document the terrain's suitability for a railroad.[52] Charles William Wilson, surveying in the Cascades and writing in his diary, also sketched views of the scenery in watercolour, although his editor claimed him less successful in the latter activity.[53] Wilson noted this pastime in his diary: "Sitting down sketching some high mountains...."[54] R. M. Rylatt's reminiscences include a number of delightful pencil sketches charmingly reproduced in the published edition. His disclaimer that, "as I was never taught drawing, surely it would be unfeeling to laugh at my efforts, be they ever so poor," was probably ritualistic, it is certainly unnecessary.[55] Prominent London lawyer Wallis Nash referred to himself as "the artist" throughout his book of travels to and from Oregon, and he is reported to have provided the illustrations for it.[56] Isabella Bird reported sketching the scenery at times in California[57] but, like Rylatt in British Columbia, professed her lack of ability to treat the colours in Colorado: "This is surely one of the most entrancing spots on earth. Oh, that I could paint with pen or brush! From my bed I look on Mirror Lake, and with the very earliest dawn, when objects are not discernible, it lies there absolutely still, a purplish lead color. Then suddenly into its mirror flash inverted peaks, at first a bright orange, then changing into red, making the dawn darker all around. This is a new sight, each morning new."[58]

Theodora Guest was another visitor whose watercolour sketches served as snapshots, capturing the scene in quick strokes: "I could only make an unfinished scratch, with a tint or two of color … but I know by previous experience what a treasure every line or touch is, when one gets home."[59] Her book is filled with engravings based on her watercolours. Another amateur artist was the Earl of Southesk, whose view of the Canadian Rockies produced "feelings almost too deep for utterance." Accordingly, he took a "rough piece of paper from [his] pocket [and] made a hasty sketch of the principal peaks."[60] His preface notes that most of the illustrations in his book, *Saskatchewan and the Rocky Mountains* (1875), are based on his own drawings.

Comparisons to specific painters and paintings were not uncommon, although it is not clear whether the writers saw the paintings on canvas or reproduced as engravings or lithographs in the press. Those who compared a landscape's colours to paintings were undoubtedly referring to the original works. William Butler, explorer and military man, likened a dramatic scene to Claude Lorraine's "Twilight in the Wilderness."[61] Miner R. Byron Johnson found one dreary

spot on B.C.'s Thompson River comparable to the work of Gustave Doré.[62] Arthur Pendarves Vivian thought a hunting scene with a wounded mountain lion was the perfect theme for painter Sir Edmund Henry Landseer.[63] Reverend George M. Grant compared one sky to Titian[64] and an oncoming storm to a work by Rosa Bonheur.[65] Later, he compared a gorge to Thomas Hill's "painting of the Yo Semite Valley."[66] Of this group, only Hill had a reputation for far western landscapes.[67]

Albert Bierstadt's western paintings were increasingly well known by 1866. Sir Charles Dilke complained upon seeing a painting of the Wind River Mountains that the painter had "caught the forms, but missed the atmosphere of the range: the clouds and mists are those of Maine and Massachusetts."[68] Arthur Vivian would disagree. His 1879 *Wanderings in the Western Land* includes a number of illustrations from Bierstadt's sketches, resulting in part from Bierstadt's patronage by Lord Dunraven, Vivian's brother-in-law.[69] At the Great Salt Lake, Vivian notes, "What a scene for Bierstadt's brush! but even he would have run the risk of being charged with exaggerating effects while only adhering truly to nature as she appeared on that beauteous morn." Elsewhere, he suggests that western nature perhaps exceeds even Bierstadt's capabilities.[70]

The increasing availability of photography affected landscape description in many ways. Reverend Grant exclaimed: "A good photographer would make a name and perhaps a fortune, if he came up here and took views. At every step we longed for a camera."[71] Grant's boss, Sir Sandford Fleming, relied on a photographer to document the terrain to be crossed by the railroad.[72] Other expeditions, British and

American, also included a photographer to document the western landscape.[73] Surveyor Charles William Wilson, for example, noted in his diary, "October 28th to 31st. [1859] Tolerably fine weather, during which I have been taking a few photographs."[74] Some of the photographs taken by the North American Boundary Commission Survey were used by naturalist John Keast Lord's publisher as the basis for the engravings that illustrate his book of travels.[75]

In a muddled diatribe against both England and America, Sir Richard Burton explains why there is no art in America. He at least did not accede to the Wildean idea that American landscape transcended art:

An American artist might extract from such scenery as Church Butte and Echo Kanyon a system of architecture as original and national as Egypt ever borrowed from her sandstone ledges, or the North of Europe from the solemn depths of her fir forests. But Art does not at present exist in America; as among their forefathers farther east, of artists they have plenty, of Art nothing. We can explain the presence of the phenomenon in England,

22. IMPORTANT AS CROSSING POINTS, MOUNTAIN PASSES ARE NAMED, IDENTIFIED, MAPPED, AND PHOTOGRAPHED.

Yellowhead Pass. William A. Baillie-Grohman. *Fifteen Years' Sport and Life in the Hunting Grounds of Western America and British Columbia* (1900). opp. p. 304. Courtesy University of Idaho Library.

where that grotesqueness and bizarrerie of taste which is observable in the uneducated, and which, despite collections and art-missions, hardly disappears in those who have studied the purest models, is the natural growth of man's senses and perceptions exposed for generation after generation to the unseen, unceasing, ever-active effect of homely objects, the desolate aspects of the long and dreary winters, and the humidity which shrouds the visible world with its gray coloring. Should any one question the fact that Art is not yet English, let him but place himself in the centre of the noblest site in Europe, Trafalgar Square, and own that no city in the civilized world ever presented such a perfect sample of barbarous incongruity.

He goes on to suggest that America's current interests lie in commerce more than art, but that its landscape may, over time, have an impact on its artistic development:

Man may not, we readily grant, expect to be a great poet because Niagara is a great cataract; yet the presence of such objects must quicken the imagination of the civilized as of the savage race that preceded him. It is true that in America the class that can devote itself exclusively to the cultivation and the study of refinement and art is still, comparatively, small; that the care of politics, the culture of science, mechanical, and theoretic, and the pursuit of cash, have at present more to hold upon the national mind than what is disposed to consider the effeminating influences of the humanizing studies; that, moreover, the efforts of youthful genius in the body corporate, as in the individual, are invariably imitative, leading through the progressive degrees of reflection and reproduction to originality.[76]

In proclaiming that nature was grander than art, Oscar Wilde concluded that there was going to be little art in the West because, "the only scenery which inspires utterance is that which man feels himself the master of. The mountains of California are so gigantic that they are not favorable to art or poetry. There are good poets in England but none in Switzerland. There the mountains are too high. Art cannot add to nature." As a consequence, Wilde did not hesitate to proclaim the Rockies as "perhaps the most beautiful part of the West."[77]

The Artist as Observer

Even the available tools for landscape description, properly and fully used, were not always sufficient to describe the Rocky Mountain West. Travellers' tales of amazing and wonderful sights have long been denied and ridiculed as too fantastic for belief. Yellowstone Park's wonders were disbelieved for half a century after they had been first reported. British travellers in the West were careful to note that the marvels they had seen might not be believed at home. As Lord Russell expressed it, "I am sure if any artist could reproduce the richness of colouring it would look to the eyes of the Old World, at least to European eyes, as exaggerated and untrue to nature."[78]

In a common formulation, the writer would note that the beauties of the West were so great that, lacking the words, perhaps it was best to leave the description to some painter. This tactic was also common among the American forty-niners who often hesitated to put on paper expressions of aesthetic sentiment.[79] The British writers seemed more convinced of the impossibility of a painter accurately capturing the scenery. And, if it could be captured, why, it would still be disbelieved. Francis Francis thought describing Yellowstone Park "an almost hopeless task; nor do the following lines pretend to convey even a glimmer of its real magnificence."[80] Earlier, he found a small pool so wonderful as to "defy description. The brush of the greatest artist, the pen of the finest writer would alike be laid down in despair, and the genius of

23–24 (OVERLEAF). TECHNOLOGICAL LIMITATIONS REQUIRED THAT THE NORTH AMERICAN BOUNDARY COMMISSION PHOTOGRAPHS HAD TO BE TRANSLATED INTO WOOD ENGRAVINGS FOR PUBLICATION.

overleaf left: Stone pyramids on the forty-ninth parallel, on left bank of the Mooyee River. North American Boundary Commission Photographs. No. 59. Courtesy Royal Engineers Corps Library Chatham, Kent, England.

overleaf right: A camp on the boundary line. John Keast Lord. *The Naturalist in Vancouver Island and British Columbia* (1866). front. v. 2. Courtesy University of Idaho Library.

man forced to bow before the power of Nature, were it tasked to convey a faithful picture of the fantastic beauty of this unearthly scene."[81] Charles William Wilson would have agreed; surveying one panorama he wrote:

From the summit, about 7500 ft above the sea, we had a magnificent view, above the limit of trees we could see the bare peaks of the Cascades all round us, many of them clothed in snow, whilst towards the west we

recognized our old friend Mount Baker raising his hoary head high above the others like a giant of old taking his rest; the tints on the mountains at sunset were such that an artist might (if he spent his whole life in the endeavor) despair of imitating.[82]

The corollary, of course, was that if an artist could in fact capture the scene, it would still be disbelieved. As conveyed by Wilson when, proclaiming nature was irreproducible by art, he suggested, "that if one saw it painted you would say it was quite unnatural & could never be the case."[83]

Major William Francis Butler earnestly argued that such disbelief would continue to be surprised; there were still many more wonders in "Nature's" cupboards:

If some painter in the exuberance of his genius had put upon canvas such a strange contrast of colours, people would have said it is not true to nature; but nature has many truths, and it takes many a long day, and not a few years' toil, to catch a tenth of them. And, my dear friend with the eye-glass – you who know all about nature in a gallery and with a catalogue – you may take my word for it.[84]

When it was impossible to reproduce the scenery in a visual manner, it was even more difficult to write about it in a descriptive fashion. The splendours of the western landscape rendered many writers speechless, or nearly so. But not the bombastic Major Butler:

Alas, how futile is it to endeavor to describe such a view! Not more wooden are the ark animals of our childhood, than the words in which man would clothe the images of that higher nature which the Almighty has graven into the shapes of lonely mountains! Put down your wooden words bit by bit; throw in colour here, a little shade there, touch it up with sky and cloud, cast about it that perfume of blossom or breeze, and in Heaven's name what does it come to after all. Can the eye wander away, away, away until it is lost in blue distance as a lark is lost in blue heaven, but the sight still drinks the beauty of the landscape, though the source of the beauty be unseen, as the source of the music which falls from the azure depths of the sky.

After exclaiming over the difficulties, Butler goes on to describe this scene from the wild interior lands of the east side of the Canadian Rockies:

That river coming out broad and glittering from the dark mountains, and vanishing into yon profound chasm with a roar which reaches up even here — billowy seas of peaks and mountains beyond number away there to south and west — that huge half dome which lifts itself above all others sharp and clear cut against the older dome of Heaven! Turn east, look out into that plain — that endless plain where pine-trees are dwarfed to speargrass and the prairie to a meadow-patch — what do see? Nothing, poor blind reader, nothing, for the blind is leading the blind; and all this boundless range of river and plain, ridge and prairie, rocky precipice and snow-capped sierra, is as much above my poor power of words as He who built this mighty nature is higher still than all.

Like many another mountain wanderer, Butler's prose converts the mountain scenery to an experience that is, if not spiritual, very much like church going. And, as he explains, in church one cannot and should not talk about it.

Ah, my friend, my reader! Let us come down from this mountain-top to our own small level again. We will upset you in an ice-rapid; [our guide] will fire at you; we will be wrecked; we will have no food; we will hunt the moose, and do anything and everything you like, — but we cannot put in words the things that we see from these lonely mountain-tops when we climb them in the sheen of evening. When you go into your church, and the organ rolls and the solemn chant floats through the lofty aisles, you do not ask your neighbor to talk to you and tell you what it is like. If he should do anything of the kind, the beadle takes him and puts him out of doors, and then the policeman takes him and puts him indoors, and he is punished for his atrocious conduct; and yet you expect me to tell you about this church, whose pillars are the mountains, whose roof is the heaven itself, whose music comes from the harp-strings which the earth has

laid over her bosom, which we call pine-trees; and from
which the hand of the Unseen draws forth a ceaseless
symphony rolling ever around the world.[85]

Rudyard Kipling found himself at a loss for
words at the Grand Canyon of the Yellowstone.
Neither he, nor any artist, could create a view
worthy of the landscape:

The cañon was burning like Troy town; but it would
burn forever, and, thank goodness, neither pen nor
brush could ever portray its splendors adequately. The
Academy would reject the picture for a chromolitho-
graph. The public would scoff at the letter-press for
Daily Telegraphese. "I will leave this thing alone," said
I; "'tis my particular property. Nobody else shall share
it with me."[86]

Although Kipling tried, in some small measure,
to share it, or at least to share his feelings about
it, he would undoubtedly have agreed with journalist S. N. Townshend's Zen-like observation
that, in some cases at least, being able to describe
the landscape meant little. "Describing scenery
such as is here, is utterly beyond the power of any
pen. Such writers as have, in their own opinion,
fully pourtrayed [*sic*] all, or even most, of its
features on paper, show conclusively that they
have never appreciated or understood them."[87]

As spellbinding as the scenery was to the
traveller, if it did not leave one speechless, it
ought to have. At Yosemite, Arthur Vivian and
his American guide, George, stared together
down upon the valley. And, while Vivian
was awestruck, George was, as he conveyed,
"irrepressible."

I could not describe this magnificent view if I would; let
that be for others capable of putting into language one
of the finest "coups-d'oeil"[88] *known to man, one of*
those which remains impressed on the mind ever after-
wards. I was really half lost in wonder and admiration
of the scene before me, it was so far beyond what I had
anticipated, so extraordinarily grand, and stupendous.
Some words expressive of my wonder at the deep gorge
below me must have escaped my lips, for my reverie was

interrupted by "Yes, sirree, quite a dig out, I guess," coming from the laconic George. What a view it was! Hundreds of feet below us was spread out the park-like bed of the valley, here not more than half-a-mile across, in which luxuriated masses of magnificent specimens of rare conifers, rhododendrons, flowering shrubs, &c., &c., amongst which wound the sparkling little Merced stream. Beyond rose the gigantic mass of grey granite called "El Capitan," presenting a perpendicular face of 3,300 feet, and over a mile in length ("quite a stone" according to the irrepressible George).[89]

With the powers of description fading, with art lacking its long-held representational ability, with mind and tongue numb from all the beauty, it was a small wonder that anything was written about the western landscape. But for most of the travellers, and not all of them were writers or artists, just having gone there and seen it was sufficient. It was something to carry back with them no matter what. And, they returned home with much more than a snapshot. As novelist Francis Francis remarked:

[Lake] Pend d'Oreille was very beautiful, and it is worth something to be able to close your eyes, and see it as I saw it on the morning that we left — as I see it now, in fact, although two thousand miles of mountain and prairie lie between us as I write.[90]

5

"This Sublime Chaos"

THE ROCKY MOUNTAIN WILDERNESS

*It is no easy matter to place an exact picture of the topography of a country before a reader:
we must, however, endeavor to do so.*[1]

This endeavour, describing the varied elements of the western landscape – the mountains, rivers, lakes, waterfalls, forests, and prairies – a variety as vast as the landscape itself, not only taxed the travellers' descriptive vocabulary, but required new comparisons, analogies, and similes. The Rockies were, or were not, like the Alps. Mountain valleys were described as gentlemen's parks. Piles of rock were likened to architectural ruins. Today, as we try to decide how much of the West should be designated as wilderness, the freshness and wonderment expressed by British travellers in their attempts to describe the landscape provide a seldom-heard perspective. Their observations, sketches, and photographs document the lost landscape of the past.

As travellers' accounts, these descriptions range from the formulaic to the dauntingly perceptive. It was to many, as sportsman W. A. Baillie-Grohman wrote about looking down on Jackson Hole, "the most sublime scenery I have ever seen."[2] As with most primary sources, they were not written for our use, but we can find,

buried among their purposes, much that is useful in recapturing a fresh approach to our western landscape.

Everlasting Sentinels

Most British travellers came to the Rocky Mountain West because of the mountains. Although they came expecting the Alps, they found something else. Not only were the Rockies not the Alps, but they were not nestled in a cozy European landscape. The contrast with the vastness of the West at times proved overwhelming. Chief Justice Charles Russell was puzzled by this: "The scenery was what I understand by 'Alpine' in its character," he stated, as if that may not have been the correct term for it.[3]

In the United States, from a distance to the east, the Rockies both surprised and disappointed the traveller. Seen from far enough away, they appeared to be small and inconspicuous. From a hundred miles away, Maurice O'Connor Morris was impressed, but not overwhelmed.

Soon after we got a grand view of the Rocky Sierra, partially capped with snow, with Pike's Peak and Long's Peak on either side, standing like sentinels keeping an everlasting watch. They did not tower so far over their surrounding brethren as I expected, considering they are among the high points of the world; but I suppose we were nearly a hundred miles, if not more, from either.[4]

The Canadian Rockies, George M. Grant noted, were unlike the Continental Divide further south in that "there was no ambiguity about these being mountains, nor about where they commenced."[5] In and among the mountains, in most places, there indeed was "no ambiguity." The ruggedness proved a formidable obstacle to all who entered. Where there were roads, they were frequently narrow and precipitous. As Rudyard Kipling wrote nervously about his stage journey into Yellowstone Park, "There was no room for any sort of accident – a shy or swerve would have dropped us sixty feet into the roaring Gardiner River."[6]

For the railroad survey teams, travel was at its most primitive. It is not surprising that for them, entering the mountains produced that emotional feeling of sublimity that both depressed and exalted. Former British Army "Serjeant" R. M. Rylatt, concessionaire for the Canadian railway survey in the early 1870s, described the scenery in terms that made the mountains seem most uninviting:

At the further extremity of this Valley the foothills cease, and immediately in front is the foot of the pass proper; guarded on either hand by mighty giants, their sides scored by deep gorges, grim with the ages of time, gloomy with the firs, which wave their w[ei]rd boughs so long as their hardy exist[e]nce can be no[u]rished, becoming dwarfed and stunted in upper air as that no[u]rishment decreases. And then the everlasting snow, where nothing vegetable can find life and sustain it. Range the eye upward still, as one stands right under these twin sister guardians, and the topmost peaks cut their way far up into the clear sky, their snowy outlines showing with delicate penciling, and as one ga[z]es, clouds of feathery snow will be seen to occasionally obscure those outlines, whirled into mid air by the wind tempests of those giddy heights.[7]

That the mountains could be "a beautiful sight" and, at the same time, "an awful scene of beauty" gives full expression to their sublimity. Yet, to these early surveyors and explorers, the dangers of mountain travel were real. R. M. Rylatt, with more grounds for concern than Yellowstone tourist Rudyard Kipling, merely hints at those dangers amid the "grand scenery" of British Columbia:

We passed some grand scenery today, and if we except the Hope Mountain, the grandest my eye ever dwelt upon. One immense giant towered high above his fellows, his spiral peaks shooting heavenward, and bristling in the clear sky, a cold, rigid sight amid the solitude, while the suns rays scintillated his pinnacles and gorges pale blue, as they played among his glaciers. Robsons peak as it is called is a beautiful sight, an awful scene of beauty, made more so as we stand gazing upward, an isolated pair of humans, in the midst of a wilderness,

with dangers past, and more to meet 'ere we can reach our kind, with dead silence all around, and a mighty chain of Snow Capped mountains on our right hand, and on our left, which, spite of their white heads, looked frowning and threatening.[8]

A more positive view of the mountain scenery was that offered by Major William F. Butler, whose unsponsored expedition into the wintry Canadian Rockies may have given him more of a need to find the mountains hospitable:

We were now in the mountains. From the low terrace along the shore they rose in stupendous masses; their lower ridges clothed in forests of huge spruce, poplar, and birch; their middle heights covered in dense thickets of spruce alone; their summits cut into a thousand varied peaks, bare of all vegetation, but bearing aloft into the sunshine 8,000 feet above us the glittering crowns of snow which, when evening stilled the breezes, shone reflected in the quiet waters, vast and motionless.

Wonderful things to look at are these white peaks, perched up so high above our world. They belong to us, yet they are not of us. The eagle links them to the earth;

the cloud carries to them the message of the sky; the ocean sends them her tempest; the air rolls her thunders beneath their brows, and launches her lightnings from their sides; the sun sends them his first greeting, and leaves them his latest kiss. Yet motionless they keep their crowns of snow, their glacier crests of jewels, and dwell among the stars heedless of time or tempest.[9]

Explorer Richard Burton, not at first burdened with any romantic feeling toward the Rockies, referred to them as a long line of "lumpy, misshapen, barren rock."[10] Later, even he managed to become enthralled by their grandeur:

That evening the Wind-River Mountains appeared in marvelous majesty. The huge purple hangings of rain-cloud in the northern sky set off their huge proportions, and gave prominence, as in a stereoscope, to their gigantic forms, and their upper heights, hoar with the frosts of ages. The mellow radiance of the setting sun diffused a charming softness over their more rugged features, defining the folds and ravines with a distinctness which deceived every idea of distance. And as the light sank behind the far western horizon, it traveled slowly up the mountain side, till, reaching the summit, it mingled its splendors with the snow — flashing and flickering for a few brief moments, then wasting them in the dark depths of the upper air. Nor was the scene less lovely in the morning hour, as the first effulgence of day fell upon the masses of dew-cloud — at this time mist always settles upon their brows — lit up the peaks, which gleamed like silver, and poured its streams of light and warmth over the broad skirts reposing upon the plain.[11]

Many travellers found the tortuous routes through the mountains disconcerting and maze-like. The obstacles often seemed so formidable to travel that there could be no forward progress. Isabella Bird noted that, "Golden City stands at the mouth of Toughcuss, otherwise Clear Creek Canyon, which many people think the grandest scenery in the mountains, as it twists and turns marvelously, and its stupendous sides are nearly perpendicular, while farther progress is to all appearance continually blocked by great masses of rock and piles of snow-covered mountains."[12]

In and among the Rockies were many little mountains among the big mountains; these vantage points overlooked the prairies and the valleys below. A climb to the top of one of the smaller peaks outside Canon City, Colorado, provided A. B. Legard with a panoramic view of the valley and its encircling mountains. He, too, thought the mountains were so enclosed as to be impassable:

Here you have before you the apparently impenetrable range of the Greenhorn Mountains. To your left is the mouth of the Oak Creek cañon. Through this gap you see, extending like the ocean, the endless prairies. Behind you is the great range, of which Pike's Peak is the most prominent feature. To your right the cañon of the Arkansas, and the great mountains through which it runs. At your feet is growing the sweetest wall-flower, and a thousand other beautiful flowers, – lovely, but scentless. To your front again, looking down the almost perpendicular cliff over which your road runs, and about one hundred feet below you, is a beautiful little green valley, nearly circular, and about a quarter of a mile in diameter, surrounded on every side by mountains hundreds of feet high. Large pine trees are growing

picturesquely here and there, and, along the left edge, a strip of cotton-wood trees and wild cherries.[13]

Such vistas from mountain peaks were not inde-scribable to these travellers. Even to the least susceptible, they cried out for description and sketching. Struck by the beauty of the landscape before him, W. A. Baillie-Grohman stopped in his tracks to note the scene in what he called "myrioramic outline," in other words, a seg-mented panoramic sketch of a scene too big to fit on one page of his notebook.

From the top an immensely vast landscape is to be seen. Standing at my horse's side and leaning over his back, using the saddle as a desk, I sketch in brief myrioramic outline the landscape, for the peak is on, on account of its isolated position, a remarkably favourable point of view. Towards the north-west I can descry the steam from the nearest Yellowstone geyser, eighty or ninety miles off, rising over a lower range of mountains. That is all I can see of the Yellowstone region, for immediately in front of me, trending Eastwards, there lies a vast sea of broken country, savagely hacked and torn by a maze of huge fissures and gloomy canyon-like valleys, from which rise an infinity of strangely-formed peaks and pinnacles. It is the weird Sierra-Shoshoné – a great ocean, as Captain Jones says, of purgatorial wave-work, having the appearance as if God's wrath had rested longer on this sublime chaos than on most other spots. There is little timber about it, save on the lower slopes, thereby increasing the forbidding look of this upheaved sea.[14]

Similarly, when S. N. Townshend took his after-breakfast stroll to the top of one hill and then another, he found himself nearing the summit of Colorado's Mount Del Norte in his carpet slippers. The view was, he wrote, "unique and charming."

The mountain top was enveloped in a mist, so was the desert valley; but Sol was rapidly getting the upper hand, and unable to continue the climb in the rarefied mountain air – which makes one gasp in a most extraordinary manner, each inspiration and expiration taking much longer than one is accustomed to – I turned round, and sat down. The mists had risen; below me was the Rio Grande del Norte (great river of the north) softly flowing in an arc southward, a broad belt of the brightest of yellow cotton wood marking its course as far as the eye could follow; under my feet the town, divided into squares by mountain streams – three large brick and about a hundred wooden houses, a puff of steam from a little saw mill on the outskirts, twenty little cabins on the plain across the river, and a few cattle dotted about them. To the east, forty miles away, the Sangre de Cristos, like mountain ptarmigan, have assumed their white winter plumage. To the west, an infinity of small valleys, branches of the great San Luis; a curl of blue smoke, and a green field in the distance among them, showing that the pushing rancher has penetrated this portion of the rocky vales. An eagle soars above me; one pine represents the timber of my mountain; fantastic-shaped cacti bloom all round. Granite rocks, stones, and pebbles browny-red, are all the mineral wealth I behold; but I must get to the summit to see if there is anything at the other side, though fifty to one there is only a higher mountain.[15]

From one of those higher mountains, Isabella Bird looked across from one peak to the range beyond. She saw no peaceful valley scene, but instead focused on the harsh forbidding landscape above the treeline, "Serrated ridges, not much lower than that on which we stood, rose, one beyond another, far as that pure atmosphere could carry the vision, broken into awful chasms deep with ice and snow, rising into pinnacles piercing the heavenly blue with their cold, barren grey, on, on for ever, till the most distant range upbore unsullied snow alone."[16]

On another expedition, she surveyed a more complex scene, yet one that ultimately was also crowned with "pure unsullied snow."

I rode up one great ascent where hills were tumbled about confusedly; and suddenly across the broad ravine, rising above the sunny grass and the deep green pines, rose in glowing and shaded red against the glittering blue heaven a magnificent and unearthly range of mountains, as shapely as could be seen, rising into colossal points, cleft by deep blue ravines, broken up by shark's teeth, with gigantic knobs and pinnacles rising from their inaccessible sides, very fair to look upon — a glowing, heavenly, unforgettable sight, and only four miles off. Mountains they looked not of this earth, but such as

one sees in dreams alone, the blessed ranges of "the land which is very far off." They were more brilliant than those incredible colors in which painters array the fiery hills of Moab and the Desert…. They were vast ranges, apparently of enormous height, their color indescribable, deepest and reddest near the pine-draped bases, then gradually softening into wonderful tenderness, till the highest summits rose all flushed, and with an illusion of transparency, so that one might believe that they were taking on the hue of sunset. Below them lay broken ravines of fantastic rocks, cleft and canyoned by the river, with a tender unearthly light over all, the apparent warmth of a glowing clime, while I on the north side was in the shadow among the pure unsullied snow.[17]

Arthur Vivian was equally struck by the vision of white snow crowning the nearby peaks. He shared with many sportsmen the feeling that one of the greatest benefits of hunting is the opportunity to get out among the scenery:

But my want of success in hunting had been much compensated by the magnificent scenery I saw this day, unsurpassed by any it had been my fortune as yet to come across. *The views from the ridges were very grand. Within a very short distance to the west, started up a grand range of mountains attaining a height of at least 13,000 feet. Dense pine-forests clothed them to within two or three thousand feet of their summits, beyond which the pure whiteness of the snow was only broken here and there by serrated masses and peaks of volcanic rock.*[18]

On another peak, Baillie-Grohman imagined that he could almost see, far to the West, the Pacific Ocean, closer to eight hundred miles away than six hundred. The clear mountain air was notoriously deceptive in its representation of distance:

A last preposterously steep slope of sharp-edged shale, on which it seemed impossible for man or beast to gain a firm foothold, and we had at last conquered that forbidding eastern face of the Big Windriver chain, and were standing on the height of land from which we saw both the Atlantic and Pacific slopes of the great continental backbone stretching away into dim distance that seemed so vast as almost to promise a glimpse of the Pacific

Ocean, quite 600 miles westwards of us. The view that burst on our eyes contrasted strangely with the one upon which we were turning our backs. For the arid, treeless steppes and bizarrely-shaped hills of bright red and yellow tints, which are the principal features of the parched mauvaise terre landscape of western Wyoming, were replaced by a glorious vista of boundless dark green forests, emerald glens and bottom lands, snow-topped mountains of grand Alpine type, at the base of which lay embosomed beautiful lakes, or flowed great rivers whose long green stretches were broken here and there by the white water of rapids.[19]

The crystalline nature of the atmosphere brought into sharp perception the colours of the rocks, trees, sky, and clouds. It also seemed as though it played tricks on the eyes. Baillie-Grohman was particularly critical of the effect of this atmospheric clarity, which was so unlike the Alps:

Peaks do not float in the air, for, so to speak, there is no air that we can see or feel. The absence of moisture in the atmosphere, while it affords vision far greater play than in other mountain landscape, is practically achromatic.

The bold buttresses and pinnacles, their snow, their shadowy ravines, their gloomy canyons, are displayed with tantalizing precision and uncompromising hardness. There is no tender play of colour, no harmonious perspective blending the near and the far. There are no great banks of airy silver-streaked billows to give depth to the picture, and to cast fairy shadows upon the mountain slopes; while the wondrous play of shifting light and shade caused by these fugitive exhalations – effects dear to the lover of European Alpine scenery – is sadly wanting.[20]

He goes on to suggest that by nightfall, or at some less stark season, the harshness of the scenery is reduced and rendered less frightening – although the latter term is not one he would have used in this context:

By moonlight these features of landscape beauty are no longer lacking. In autumn, when the days are warm and the nights very cold, filmy vapour not unfrequently rises after dark. The summits of the mountains rear their glittering heads from the gauzy clouds of it, while the subdued and silvery light of the brilliant moon is chary of invading the gorges and ravines. There is light, there is shade, there is tender perspective. The stark rocks and austerely colourless backgrounds are lost in mysterious half-distances, and an air of tranquil, romantic beauty is cast over scenery, which at other times chills you by its raw vastness.[21]

The multi-hued colours of the Western scenery were often mentioned; Isabella Bird noted that, "for color, the Rocky Mountains beat all I have seen."[22] George M. Grant suggested that the colours amid the rocky gyrations were so varied as to keep an artist occupied for some time:

Not only the dark green of the spruce in the corries, which turned into black when far up, but autumn tints of red and gold as high as vegetation had climbed up the hillsides; and above that, streaks and patches of yellow, green, rusty red, and black relieving the grey mass of limestone; while up in the valley, every shade of blue came out according as the hills were near or far away, and summits hoary with snow bounded the horizon.[23]

Whether describing the inland passage between Vancouver Island and the Coast Range or the interior between the Cascade Mountains and the Northern Rockies, it was easy to say, as did sportsman John Turner-Turner, that "the usual picture of British Columbian scenery [is] – mountains, mountains, and nothing but mountains."[24] In other regions, the landscape showed more variation. Turner-Turner thought the mountains of British Columbia were less monotonous than the American scenery where he had hunted,[25] but this view was not shared by Baillie-Grohman. In Wyoming, for example, Baillie-Grohman ranged through diverse high-elevation scenery on his hunting expeditions. In this summary of his travels, he specifically refers to its Alp-like, yet varied, character:

For more than four months we roamed over incomparable mountain territory, for weeks camped at altitudes varying between 10,000 and 12,000 feet over the sea-level – to-day perhaps on the borders of one of the hundreds of small exquisitely-beautiful mountain tarns that dot the great backbone of the Big Wind River Mountains; tomorrow at the brink of a deep gloomy canyon, of mysterious depth and supreme grandeur; while on the following day, night would surprise us close to Timberline, in the dense green wilderness of the pathless forests of the Western slopes, where we would spread our robes under the broad branches of a stately silver pine; the following evening's camp-fire lighting up great fantastically-shaped and grotesquely-coloured walls of rock, closing in on every side a small emerald-tinted meadow lining the bank of a turbulent mountain stream, to which snug cliff-bowered retreat access could only be gained by following the beaver's example, and wading our horses through the gloomy canyons the waters had worn through the surrounding mountains. A couple of weeks hence we would probably be a couple of hundred miles away, threading our way through the grotesque mauvaises terres scenery, grandly coloured, and of the superbly bizarre formation, by which the Sierra Soshoné [sic], that unexplored sea of nameless peaks cut by deep gorges of tortuous course, is distinguished. Every day, every hour, new scenery, new vistas of Alpine landscape, burst upon our eyes.[26]

To many, the mountains were, of course, as much spiritual as physical entities. The personification of "Nature" in general, and mountains in particular, led to such effusions as George M. Grant's on the regenerative nature of mountain wilderness:

There was nothing fantastic about the mountain forms. Everything was imposing. And these too were ours, an inheritance as precious, if not as plentiful in corn and milk, as the rich plains they guarded. For mountains elevate the mind, and give an inspiration of courage and dignity to the hardy races who own them and breathe their atmosphere.[27]

Valleys and Parks

From the mountain peaks, even minor peaks, travellers could often see tantalizing glimpses of additional mountains, park-like valleys, and slowly meandering rivers. Within the mountains, they found precipitous cliffs, plateaus interspersed with crevasses, and sharp gorges made frantic with the rapidly running water of a mountain torrent. R. M. Rylatt, reminisced on "one of the wildest and grandest scenes in nature."

What a view bursts on the sight from the summit of Hope Mountain; while standing on its broad flat crown, the vision takes in one of the wildest and grandest scenes in nature, down, down in the far depths, so deep in some of the immense gorges, that night seems to eternally dwell there; while in their depths are roaring cascades, heard by none, and in appearance tiny threads of silver. The dark firs bristling from the base to the snow line, overhanging and waving their branches from giddy heights, in solitude which may never be broken; above all are the glistening summits as the sun plays upon them, and 'erewhiles canop[i]ed by whirling snow clouds as the fierce tempests strike them, for they are for ever hooded in snow, and their rugged sides varied by dark lines, or pale blue, where immense glaciers of solid ice choke them, the birthplaces of the rushing angry waters of the Cascades.[28]

The green, flat valleys nestled among the mountains often evoked to other British travellers, as it did to Rylatt, "the Parks of the rich in dear old England."[29] Isabella Bird, on the other hand, thought the "parks" were very different from those in England but a perfect setting for the enclosing mountains:

I cannot by any words give you an idea of scenery so different from any that you or I have ever seen. This is an upland valley of grass and flowers, of glades and sloping lawns, and cherry-fringed beds of dry streams, and clumps of pines artistically placed, and mountain sides densely pine clad, the pines breaking into fringes as they come down upon the "park," and the mountains breaking into pinnacles of bold grey rock as they pierce the blue of the sky. A single dell of bright green grass, on which dwarf clumps of the scarlet poison oak look like beds of geraniums, slopes towards the west, as if it must lead to the river which we seek. Deep, vast canyons, all trending westwards, lie in purple gloom. Pine-clad ranges, rising into the blasted top of Storm Peak, all run westwards too, and all the beauty and glory are but the frame out of which rises – heaven-piercing, pure in its pearly luster, as glorious a mountain as the sun tinges red in either hemisphere – , the splintered, pinnacled, lonely, ghastly, imposing, double-peaked summit of Long's Peak, the Mont Blanc of Northern Colorado.[30]

Two of the most well known among such valleys in the Rocky Mountains were Jackson Hole and Estes Park. Jackson Hole was famous as one of the midsummer rendezvous sites for the early fur traders. Here, they met to exchange the winter's catch of furs for supplies and whiskey. By 1880, when Baillie-Grohman passed through the area on his hunting trip, Jackson Hole had regained its tranquil sublimity, and suffered no more from the raucous shouts of carousing mountain men.

At our feet lay the perfectly level expanse, about eight or ten miles broad, and five-and-twenty in length. Traversing the basin lengthwise, we saw the curves of the Snake River – its waters of a beautiful beryl green, and apparently as we viewed it, from a distance of five or six miles, of glassy smoothness – winding its way through groves of stately old cottonwood trees. A month or two before, the Snake had inundated the whole basin, and the grass that had sprung up retained its bright green tint, giving the whole picture the air of splendid trimly-kept old park. Beyond the river, the eye espied several little lakes, nestling in the forest-girt seclusion under the beetling cliffs of the boldest-shaped mountain I am acquainted with, i.e. the Grand Teton Peak, rising in one great sweep from an amazingly serrated chain of aiguille-like crags sharply outlined against the heavens, and shutting in one entire half of the basin, – the other semicircular enclosure being the mountain range on which we stood.[31]

To the early fur traders, a "hole" was a flattish valley in and among the mountains that was used for pasturage and an annual rendezvous. Jackson Hole, today, while still surrounded by mountains, is a place of multi-million-dollar homes and ski resorts, much changed from Baillie-Grohman's description.

Estes Park had, and still has, a much different association, although a park was much the same as a hole. To most British travellers, Estes Park was Lord Dunraven's private hunting preserve. A hotel and other accommodations made it a prime vacation area during Denver's hot summer months as well as staging ground for visiting sportsmen. Arthur Vivian, Lord Dunraven's brother-in-law, was forthright in his approval of the venture and the locale:

Higher and higher we get as we slowly perform the journey by the simple but sure process of more ups than downs, until at length we reached the ridge above Estes park, and looked down upon this lovely basin with the grand encircling mountains beyond. The beauty of this view must be seen to be appreciated; even such an artist as Bierstadt, who is certainly the happiest I have seen in depicting American scenery, could not do justice to this bewitching coup-d'oeil. *The "Park" lies below us, like a well-kept pleasure ground, about a couple of miles in breadth, and ten or twelve miles long. Running up from it into the range are many little glens, some pretty long and broad, others mere "gulches," but none extending more than six or eight miles before the mountain sides are reached. The encircling range on the left of our view can boast of Long's Peak, which is 14,271 feet above the sea level, and the highest point in the park; but the peaks opposite are within a thousand feet of it, and have equally enchanting outlines. The loveliness of the scene is much enhanced by the brightness of the green of the park itself, which, although in marked contrast with the grim and sombre crags of the mountains beyond, seems to pass away to them in perfect harmony through the medium of the pine-covered sides. The trees grow as high up as a 12,000 feet elevation, beyond which are the bare ragged masses of volcanic rocks towering up two or three thousand feet more. Truly, the introduction to Estes park is a lovely one.*[32]

Today, half the scenery in Estes Park is protected through its inclusion in Rocky Mountain National Park. Although the mountains still surround it, much of the eastward plain has been turned into suburban ranchettes, stretching from Fort Collins to Denver.

Richard Byron Johnson, a British Columbia gold miner, described another park-like scene in a more remote region, above where the Thompson flows into the Fraser River. The park-like meadows were a stark contrast to the sheer walls of the surrounding mountains, which appeared to sit right at the edge of the valley:

We were far away from the haunts of white men, and were alone with Nature in its grand primeval beauty. The river began to spread itself into a large stream, marked in its course by piles of bleached drift-wood, in a valley whose width was correspondingly increased. Natural meadows extended for a few miles on either bank till they met the sides of the mountain ridges, clothed with huge fir and spruce-trees sloping mist-ily upwards in the purple distance, till the vegetation gradually decreased in size and density, and ultimately became lost in the regions of eternal snow, where naught disturbed the sameness of the great horizon of blinding whiteness save a few jagged black peaks too steep for the feathery substance to light upon; and far away to the eastward, in the clear mountain air, could be seen the stupendous and fantastic summits of the Rocky Mountains.[33]

For many travellers, the sight of such apparently unoccupied park-like land raised visions of farms, homes, and livestock. S. N. Townshend, noting the availability of homesteading rights to naturalized citizens, proclaimed the virtues of one such Colorado valley. British subjects, and others eligible for citizenship, were able to claim homestead lands providing they certified their intent to become citizens.

The head of this gulch opens into a beautiful sweeping valley, from the head of which the Sangre de Cristo range shows very imposingly. What a spot for residences this fine natural park would make! Fifteen peaks, 10,000 feet to 13,000 feet high, tower above it; glades, dells, smooth sloping lawns, thickets, clumps, and single trees are scattered about, now thickly, now thinly, here enclosing 20 acres, there 1000. If any man wants to plant with taste, let him study nature here; not one foot of this land is taken up, it is all to be had for the asking by naturalised citizens. The society offered by the district is at present deer, bear, and grouse; but "the Switzerland of America" spreads all her natural charms to entice the stranger hither, and retain him when caught; and the wonder is that only Lord Dunraven has, from the eastern world, picked up "for a song" a park in the western Hemisphere which laughs to scorn the beauties of home ones.[34]

However scenic it might be, Townshend goes on to warn of the consequences of considering such park-like areas adequate as range lands, "True, these parks are very useless save for sport and health; ten thousand acres of them will not feed as many cattle as five hundred Kansas acres."[35] This is a lesson still to be learned on much of our western range.

Deep, Vast Canyons

The opposite of placid valleys must surely be rugged canyons. Whether gorges, ravines, gulches, or chasms, the earth's declivities evoked strong words from the traveller. Making his way through the mountains by train, Robert Louis Stevenson found the Colorado canyons "sterile"[36] while in the Sierras, a "glimpse of a huge pine-forested ravine upon my left, a foaming river, and a sky already coloured with the fires of dawn" prompted him to declare, "I am usually very calm over the displays of nature; but you will scarce believe how my heart lept at this."[37] To others, the bare rock walls evoked different sensations. Novelist George A. Lawrence was not nearly as affected:

An artist's eye might find attractions here, even at this dreary season; though the sternness of the huge cliff-walls on either hand is enhanced rather than softened by the fringes of stunted pines, clinging and climbing where-ever they can find foot-hold; and there are studies for the geologist, in the rapid and abrupt changes of "formations" wherever the rocks stand out bare.[38]

It was in formidable, rocky country such as this that Lawrence noted their "savage grandeur."[39] The ruggedness of the country in places is still formidable. Baillie-Grohman found the narrow canyons in the Teton Range quite remarkable: "They are often so narrow that you come upon them with startling abruptness, and look down yawning gorges two and three thousand feet deep, and at the top only half that width. They are undoubtedly finer than anything we have in the Alps."[40] Isabella Bird indirectly provided an example of this rugged character: "The stillness is profound. I hear nothing but the far-off mysterious roaring of a river in a deep canyon, which we spent two hours last night in trying to find."[41] Another hunter, near the Big Horn River in Wyoming, warned of the hazards of travel in such convoluted geography:

The scenery throughout was wildly picturesque and grand, with cañons of such formations as to render the crossing of them without a guide impossible, a detour of ten miles being frequently necessary to reach a particular trail. A party in our vicinity managed to arrive at the bottom of one of these cañons, but by no possible means did they find themselves able, either to return by the way they had entered, or escape on the other side, the upshot being that their hunter was forced to seek the aid of someone acquainted with the locality to extricate the outfit, which remained imprisoned many days.[42]

Such steep gorges and maze-like trails were compounded by the immense depth and narrowness of the canyons. The surveyors were much hindered at times when they needed to see the sun with their instruments. Charles Wilson noted, "In one place where observations were taken for altitude, the sun was only visible for 3 hours in the day, the huge precipices literally hanging over you & the mountain torrent rushing along at your feet."[43] The steep canyon walls may have interfered with their scientific observations, but the landscape also provided moments of rare beauty. "On getting up in the morning at about five we had a beautiful sight, the deep gorge we were in, being still in the dark shade of the night, with the moon shining gloriously overhead, whilst the high peaks around us were tipped with the bright gold of the rising sun."[44]

Others found the canyons much more visually impressive than the flat valleys. A. B. Legard, in his report on Colorado, contrasted the rocky traverse of a deep canyon with one of the park-like valleys:

Descending into this little valley, and riding for about a quarter of a mile under the shade of the pine trees, which scent the air with their peculiarly refreshing smell, you come to the mouth of a great mountain gorge, which you would think no living creature could penetrate. The granite walls rise perpendicularly for hundreds of feet on both sides. You are surrounded by wild cherry trees, whose sweet blossoms scent the whole air. At your feet runs a clear, rushing, gurgling mountain stream. It is here that you enter the cañon of Oak Creek, following up the course of the stream, crossing it every five minutes, cramming your way through the undergrowth of scrubby oak and wild cherries. Through these walls your road runs for eight miles, and then again opens on to a grassy valley, but of no particular beauty.[45]

So Great a River

Water in the West has always been contentious; there is either too much of it or not enough of it. Paradoxically, some arid regions, lacking measurable precipitation, have immense rivers flowing through them. Such rivers may have banks so precipitous that it is impossible to reach the water swirling far below. Navigation by raft or canoe is made even more difficult by waterfalls and rapids, where the water's immense flows are channelled over and between huge boulders. George M. Grant described the near fatal adventures of one group travelling in British Columbia:

A party of gentlemen ignorant of the geography of the country, and deserted by their guides in endeavoring to cross the Rocky Mountains a few years ago, further south, argued similarly when they struck the Columbia River. "So great a river cannot go wrong: its course must be the best; let us follow it to the sea." And they did follow its northerly sweep round the Kootanie or Selkirk mountains, for one or two hundred miles, till inextricably entangled among fallen timber, and cedar swamps, they resolved to kill their horses, make rafts or canoes, and trust to the river. Had they carried this plan out, they would have perished, for no raft or canoe can get through the terrible canyons of the Columbia.

But fortunately two Suswap Indians came upon them at this juncture, and though not speaking a word that they knew, made them understand by signs, that their only safety was in retracing their steps, and by getting round the head waters of the Columbia, reach Fort Colville by the Kootanie Pass.[46]

Similarly, among the same northern wilds of the Rockies, Major Butler described a portage where water travellers took to land to avoid the dangerous rapids. This involved removing everything from the canoe and making several trips around the hazard, carrying all of the goods and luggage, often through terrain that was likewise nearly impassable. The final step was to transport the canoe, either by roping it through the rapids or carrying it overland:

Some fifty miles west of St. John, the Peace River issues from the cañon through which it passes the outer range of the Rocky Mountains. No boat, canoe, or craft of any kind has ever run the gauntlet of this huge chasm; for five-and-thirty miles it lies deep sunken through the mountains; while from its depths there ever rises the hoarse roar of the angry waters as they dash furiously against their rocky prison. A trail of ten miles leads across this portage, and at the western end of this trail the river is reached close to where is makes its first plunge into the rock-hewn chasm. At this point the traveller stands within the outer range of the mountains, and he

27. RIVERS WERE THE ROADS IN THE EARLY WEST — PEOPLE TRAVELLED BY BOAT IN THE SUMMER OR ON THE ICE IN THE WINTER.

Up the Skeena River. J. Turner-Turner. *Three Years' Hunting and Trapping in America and the Great North-West.* (1888). p. 72. Courtesy University of Idaho Library.

has before him a broad river, stretching far into a region of lofty peaks, a river with strong but even current, flowing between banks 200 to 300 yards apart. Around great mountains lift up their heads dazzling with the glare of snow, 10,000 feet above the water which carries his frail canoe.[47]

John Turner-Turner, and his wife, "L.," spent the greater part of 1887 and 1888 hunting and trapping in the interior of British Columbia. On leaving their isolated camp, they suffered several mishaps as they travelled by Native canoe down

the Fraser River. The first of the mishaps was the overturning of their canoe after they had packed the heavier items around the rapids:

We reached Fort George Cañon the first day, and after packing all the heavy articles, the Indians took a few light things in the canoe, and proceeded to run the cañon; the water was a bit worse than they had supposed, and they were all but capsized. Several things were thrown out, including, of course, that which could never be replaced, namely, all the notes we had taken during our trip, together with L.'s diary; by great good luck, however, the box floated, and was rescued, while the contents were quickly laid out in the sun to dry.[48]

The next adventure occurred when the couple decided to run the rapids fully loaded rather than break up the load and portage part of it as they had done previously:

Next morning we started about five o'clock, the river had risen considerably in the night; and about midday we came in sight of a particularly bad-looking piece of water where the waves were rolling and dashing up stream to an alarming height. "How shall you pass that?" I said to Johnnie. "All right this side, good water here," he replied; but when he came within sight of what he had relied on as good water, he cried out, "no good;" and then calling out in an excited tone to the other Indian, the canoe was turned towards the opposite shore, and the two struggled with all their might. I needed not to glance at the faces of the panic-stricken Indians, pale with fear, and painfully distorted in their frantic efforts to propel the heavily loaded canoe free of danger. The magnitude of the peril was too apparent to require such demonstration; and at that moment while we were rapidly drifting into the very centre of the boiling mass, across which the canoe scarcely seemed to gain an inch, I would have laid fifty to one against the chances of any one of us; as for poor L. there was often a stage at which she became speechless, for those few minutes no power on earth could have loosened her tongue. Had I been able to reach the spare paddle the odds against us would have been greatly reduced, but in such water I dared not move to secure it, for the waves were already topping the gunwale, and it seemed impossible that we could escape. Like lightning we were swept along the margin of the boil, and down lay the Indians in the

bottom of the canoe, lest the heavy roll should capsize
her. We had escaped, but it was a narrow shave, and the
greedy Fraser rarely gives up its victims even when their
destruction is complete.[49]

At the next rapids, they determined to portage
rather than risk it all again. This turned out to be
equally as strenuous:

All things had been removed from the canoe and taken
over the cañon to the landing at the opposite end, and
next morning came the question of how to get the canoe
up the precipitous rocks, which in one spot were almost
perpendicular for about seventy feet. Johnnie said there
were Chinamen mining close by who would help us; but
on consulting them they refused to lend a hand under
$15, this I declined to pay them, telling Johnnie we
would do it ourselves; but after an hour's struggle we
had only accomplished about eighty yards of the easiest
part, and clearly saw that the remainder was an impos-
sibility. I therefore sent to the Chinamen, offering $10,
which they accepted, and in about an hour and a half
more, we got the canoe over and down the other side of
the cañon.[50]

For all its hazards, the Fraser River canyon had
its attractions. Gold miner R. B. Johnson thought
the Thompson River, by comparison, was much
worse. "Of all the dismal and dreary-looking
places in the world, the valley of the Thompson
River, for some fifteen or twenty miles from
its mouth, would easily take the palm. We had
thought the *cañons* of the Fraser rugged enough;
but here was nought but rocks, whereon even
the hardy fir refused to vegetate."[51] Not all of the
scenery near the Thompson was as repulsive, he
noted, "On reaching the summit I could not help
exclaiming with admiration on the magnificence
of the picture spread beneath and around. To the
eastwards wound a long and wide valley, on the
other side of which were the mountains which
hid the North Fork of the Thompson River from
us."[52] Others found the latter more attractive:

There was a bend in the river to the west, so that we
saw not only a little up and down, which is usually all
that can be seen on the North Thompson, but round the
corner; a wide extent of landscape of varied beauty and
soft outlines. The hills were wooded, and the summits of

the highest dusted with the recent snow, that had been
rain-fall in the valley. Autumn hues of birch, cotton-
wood, and poplar blended with the dark fir and pine,
giving the variety and warmth of colour that we had for
many days been strangers to, and which was therefore
appreciated all the more.[53]

Sometimes, it all depended on the previous experience used for comparison. Of the Little Blue
River in Nebraska, explorer Richard Burton
humorously suggested that, "its beauties require
the cosmetic which is said to act unfailingly in
the case of fairer things – the viewer should have
lately spent three months at sea, out of sight of
rivers and women."[54]

Different rivers evoked different responses.
Arthur Vivian found the Platte's canyons "difficult to equal in wildness, grandeur, and desolation."[55] For naturalist John Keast Lord, the Snake
River, near its conjunction with the Columbia
River, was surrounded by "immense walls of
rocks." He reported that the scenery was "bare,
black, and desolate; not a tree or shrub grows
from amidst their craggy ledges. I am told the

course of this river may be followed for days
in some places, and by no means can its waters
be reached, so that one might die from thirst
although on the bank of a river."[56]

Near the same area, above the Touchet River,
Lord's companion, Charles Wilson, found that,
"we had a wonderful if not a beautiful view; far
below us ran the little stream through a narrow
gorge with a brilliant streak of green on its
banks; the only sign of vegetation that could be
seen; far as the eye could reach nothing could be
seen but a succession of those wonderful rolling
hills, covered with dry bunch grass, which I can
hardly give you an idea of, unless you can imagine yourself looking down on a sea of land with
a heavy ground swell immensely magnified."[57]
The rivers of the West encompassed a variety of
waters and the surrounding scenery ranged from
small freshets to mighty torrents. As Baillie-
Grohman noted:

Western rivers are all very arbitrary and self-willed
powers in the land. Many have a bad name for most
dangerous quicksands, others for their extraordinarily

Mountains So Sublime

rapid rise. Some of the larger creeks in the northern "bad-lands" are known to rise twenty and thirty feet in half an hour, in consequence of rainstorms. Again, others take it into their heads to sink out of sight just when their precious liquid is most wanted, and keep out of man's way for ten or twenty, in places even for sixty, miles. I know not of one single river or stream west of the Missouri that has not some more or less memorable awkward quality or characteristic about it....[58]

A Lake Smooth as a Mirror

If flowing water provided both scenery and trepidation, the lakes in the West ranged from the picturesque to the dull. The more common postcard image of a western lake is that of W. A. Baillie-Grohman's description of Kootenai Lake:

It was a glorious June afternoon when we glided out of the tree-bowered mouth of the river, and saw before us the lake. One could see almost to the end of the mirror-like sheet, in which the row of peaks on both sides, still capped with snow, were reflected most effectively. Over the whole scene lay the charm of absolute wildness and solitude, for not a single white dweller and only a few roaming Indians lived on its shores.[59]

Similarly, Francis Francis was enthralled by the reflective qualities of a small lake in the wilderness. "Each pool is a mirror. In its pure depths the fleecy clouds reflected sail slowly by, the dainty biscuit-work of the fountain's edges is faithfully reproduced, and the beholder himself, as he gazes therein, is photographed with a clearness that is at first sight startling."[60] Francis was particularly struck by the variety presented by this colourful Yellowstone scene's shades and hues magnified, as it were, by being reflected in the still water.

It is impossible to conceive anything more beautiful than the colouring here presented. The water is of the purest, brightest cerulean hue, but near the shallow edges it takes its tone from the enclosing rocks, and the glorious azure is lost in yellow, pale green, or red, whilst chemical deposits, in exquisite arrangements, such as

*the genius of Nature alone can suggest, of écru and
ivory, lemon and orange, buff, chocolate, brown, pink,
vermillion, bronze, and fawn encircle the pool, or paint
with ribbon-like effect the tiny streams that trickle from
its overflow.*[61]

George Grant also commented on the reflections
of the various colours of the rocks. "A little further on, another lakelet reflected the mountains
to the right, showing not only the massive grey
and blue of the limestone, but red and green
colourings among the shales that separated the
strata of limestone."[62]

John Keast Lord, declaring himself "not so
much impressed with the beauty of the landscape, as awed by its substantial magnificence,"
found, in this excerpt, that the stillness of the
lake concealed its great depths. The glassy surface
hid more than it revealed:

*The sun had crept steadily up into the clear sky,
unflecked by a single cloud; the mists, that in the early
morning hung about the ravines, and partially veiled the
peaks and angles of the vast piles of rocks, had vanished,
revealing them in all their immensity. Below me was a
lake, smooth as a mirror, but the dark-green cold look of
the water hinted at unfathomable depth. Tiny rivulets,
fed by the snow, wound their way, like threads of silver,
between the rocks and through the grass, to reach the
lake.*[63]

Strange as it may seem, not all western lakes
were citadels of great beauty. In interior British
Columbia, John Turner-Turner declared that
Babine Lake was "a most uninteresting piece of
water, with not a scrap of picturesque scenery to

relieve its monotony save at the southern extremity, where the surroundings became mountainous, and the quaint bottle-necked nests of the cliff-swallows were clustered in hundreds over the bluff rocks." This dismissal may be a consequence of his having travelled by canoe over the entire one hundred miles of its length.[64]

Charles Wilson, travelling through what is now part of northeastern Washington, also found a lake that did not incite him to extol its beauty. "Shortly after leaving Leyenbeel creek we came to a large lake & kept along it for some distance; it looked a very desolate kind of place, the basaltic cliffs in some places & the tall reeds which the breeze was just moving with a melancholy noise added to the almost total absence of life, save a few divers & one eagle who was peering at us from the top of a rock; it looked to me just the sort of place where a murder might be committed or any atrocity, unnoticed & unknown."[65]

Lawyer Wallis Nash gave some measure of notice to one of the great bodies of water in the West, the seemingly lifeless Great Salt Lake. Seen from the train it was a spectacular sight:

Turning North, the line skirts the Great Salt Lake. As we saw it, a more lovely scene the eye never rested on. The fore-shore of the lake was green with grass and weed, with lines of shining water everywhere catching the evening light. The sun, sinking towards the snowy range of mountains on the Western side of the lake, sent quivering rays across its waters, while purple and orange clouds were piled up high above the horizon.[66]

Falling Waters

With water pooling in lakes and rushing over cataracts, it is not unusual to find waterfalls described among the traveller's narratives. Some were fine wispy falls such as the famed Bridal Veil Falls near the Columbia River reported by Rudyard Kipling. He wrote of "a waterfall – a blown thread of white vapor that broke from the crest of the hill – a waterfall eight hundred and fifty feet high whose voice was even louder than the voice of the river."[67] Others were more like the massive thundering cataract of Shoshone Falls on the Snake River. John Mortimer Murphy went out of his way to view the Shoshone Falls, as did many travellers on the nearby Oregon Trail. However, he described the falls less and his emotions more, when he wrote:

Selecting a mossy bank covered with a long, dank, and prostrate grass, I threw myself upon it, and for two hours gazed upon the stirring scene before me in a sort of half-dreamy mood, for it was far too overpowering to allow the faculties to expand into full action. The longer I looked the more I desired to, for I was fairly captivated by the grand yet weird beauty that surrounded me.[68]

Explorer Henry M. Stanley, then a newspaper reporter, found a charming scene in a small waterfall; "a sparkling streamlet ... [which] forms a slight cascade as it falls over a bed of quartz of snowy whiteness."[69] On a larger scale, naturalist John Keast Lord's description of Palouse Falls in eastern Washington is at first thorough and realistic. First, he describes the narrowing width of the river walled in by rocks and leading to the plunging depth of the falls, and then he adds, in

much the same fashion as Murphy, "I am ... awed and ... absorbed and lost in its wonder."[70]

Primeval Forest

Among the mountains and surrounding the waters one frequently finds immense stands of trees, the grand evergreen forests of the West. Although it is often assumed that most of the Rocky Mountain West is densely forested, this is untrue. While evergreens predominate, the West's deciduous forests can rival New England's famed fall foliage. Maurice Morris painted one such multi-coloured scene:

Nothing could exceed the beauty of the colouring of the low hills we passed "en chemin" today; under foot the leaves were many hued – but a bright scarlet predominated – then the currant and wild-cherry bushes wore an orange scarlet livery; while willows and aspens bore every conceivable tint of yellow, orange and brown, with an admixture of pale green; and then in the high background were the dark unvarying hues of the green pine, forming a frame for the picture.[71]

Chief Justice Russell saw the forests as "primeval" on the one hand and as "plantations" on the other. In any event, "against the evening sky they look at times exceedingly picturesque standing like sentinels on guard."[72] Similarly, Arthur Vivian delighted in the subtle hues of the California woods.

The beauty of the views from the ridges, embracing miles of dark foliage stretching to the plains beyond, and terminating only with the distant mountain ranges, must be seen to be understood. The colouring of the landscape on that lovely evening was enchanting, and such as I had never seen before; it ranged from the almost black green of the timber-covered foreground to a light cobalt on the far-distant mountains, each tint so striking in itself yet so toned down by nature's delicate hand as to be deliciously soft and harmonious as a whole.[73]

What we now call the "mature forest" is but one stage in a forest's natural progression. George M. Grant recognized a haunting beauty among British Columbia's fallen monarchs:

The forest is of the grandest kind – not only the living but the dead. Everywhere around lie the prostrate forms of old giants, in every stage of decay, some of them six to eight feet through, and an [sic] hundred and fifty to two hundred feet in length. Scarcely half-hiding these are broad-leaved plants and ferns in infinite variety, while the branchless columnar shafts of more modern cedars tower far up among the dark branches of spruce and hemlock, dwarfing the horse and his rider, that creep along across their interlaced roots and the mouldering bones of their great predecessors.[74]

Unpeopled Prairies

Edging up to the mountains were the prairies, the low, rolling plains that provided a setting for the mountains to frame. Unlike the peaks that hemmed in the sky, the prairie was open, almost devoid of features. Seemingly boundless, it was so vast as to be almost disorienting. Wallis

Nash noted the lack of boundaries, "Neither hedge, nor fence, nor road, nor line of trees was in sight, and the vast grass-covered undulations stretched away till the nearer features became quite indistinguishable in the limitless distance."[75] In some places, at the upper reaches, there was little to distinguish the plains from the mountains. Charles W. Dilke, travelling over the Continental Divide above Denver, noted that, "the scenery was tame enough, but strange in the extreme. Its characteristic feature was its breadth. No longer the rocky defiles of Virginia Dale, no longer the glimpses of the main range as from Laramie Plains and the foot hills of Meridian Bow, but great rolling downs like those of the Plains much magnified. We crossed one of the highest passes in the world without seeing snow, but looked back directly we were through it on snow-fields behind us and all around."[76]

Smaller prairies had their own beauty. On the Sumas prairie near Puget Sound, John Keast Lord saw "the prairie bright and lovely; the grass fresh, green, and waving lazily; various wild flowers, peeping coyly out from their cosy hiding-places, seem making the most of the summer."[77] Like the "parks," these grassy prairies appeared to invite real estate development. As George Grant exclaimed near the South Saskatchewan River, "where hundreds of homesteads shall yet be there is not one. Perhaps it is not to be regretted that there is so much good land in the world still unoccupied."[78]

Atmospheric Conditions

Accustomed to London's gritty fogs, many British travellers ascribed positive health benefits to the clear, clean atmosphere of the Rocky Mountain West. In addition, at the higher elevations, the atmosphere was made more precious by being thinner. W. A. Baillie-Grohman suggested that, thin as it was, it must carry more oxygen:

Whatever may be the demerits of the West in the eyes of some, no one has ever dared to question the amazingly inspiriting qualities of the atmosphere of these trans-Missourian highlands. Dry and sparkling as perhaps none other on the globe, it seems to be composed not of one-fifth, but of five-fifths of oxygen. As your city-worn lungs inhale it, fresh life is infused into your whole being, and you feel that it is air which has never before been breathed.[79]

As remarkable as was the scenery in the great West, it was often the weather that enhanced it. Charles Dilke, in Denver, watched the afternoon thunderclouds build up against the Front Range. "'This is a great country, sir,' said a Coloradan to me to-day. 'We make clouds for the whole universe.'"[80]

Such thunderstorms were in themselves awe inspiring, if not horrifying. Francis Francis thought that, "the wild character of the scene was enhanced" by lightning storms.[81] S. N. Townshend found the lightning around Pike's Peak so fine that, "it was long ere we could bring ourselves to retire from viewing so grand a sight."[82]

The storms added colour, in hues of gray or red, to the scenery as well, even though they may not have been the sole source of colour. George

M. Grant, dropping in altitude from the mountains to British Columbia's south Thompson River valley, noticed the gradations in atmosphere and the scenic beauty, a consequence of the mountain's rain shadow, which diminished the promised precipitation:

As we drew nearer Kamloops, characteristics of a different climate could be noted with increasing distinctness. A milder atmosphere, softer skies, easy rolling hills; but the total absence of underbrush and the dry grey grass everywhere covering the ground were the most striking differences to us, accustomed so long to the broad-leaved underbrush and dark-green foliage of the humid upper country. We had clearly left the high rainy, and entered the lower arid, region. The clouds from the Pacific are intercepted by the Cascades, and only those that soar like soap-bubbles over their summits pass on to the east. These float over the intervening country till they come to a region high enough to intercept them. Thus it is that while clouds hang over Kamloops and its neighborhood, little rain or snow falls. The only timber in the district is a knotty red pine, and as the trees grow widely apart, and the bunch-grass underneath is clean, unmixed with weeds and shrubs, and uniform in colour, the country has a well-kept park-like appearance, though there is too little of fresh green and too many signs of aridity for beauty.[83]

Most of the travellers avoided the high mountain areas during the bitterly cold winter months, but some, especially the surveyors, found themselves trapped there. In his diary, Charles Wilson joked about the extremely bad weather they suffered in early November 1859: "The thermometer went down to 12° last night & did not rise above 20° all day, which made it dreadfully cold & would almost have blown me out of bed if I had not been anchored by my hair being frozen to the pillow."[84]

Despite the cold months, even survey secretary Wilson found the western sunsets to be spectacular. On the sea-like Spokane plains, he wrote: "We had the most beautiful sunset I ever saw on shore, the sun going down over the plain behind a bank of clouds, bringing out the edges as if they had been carved with a knife & tipping them with points of gold."[85] Richard Burton,

in Wyoming, noted the effect of the afternoon breeze. "About an hour afterward the west wind, here almost invariable, brought up a shower of rain, and swept a vast veil over the forms of the Wind-River Mountains. Toward sunset it cleared away, and the departing luminary poured a flood of gold upon the majestic pile – I have seldom seen a view more beautiful."[86]

Lord Dunraven, commenting on a "lurid" sunset, wrote that, "stormy American sunsets are startling, barbaric, even savage." More surprising to him was that, "such effects could be produced at all, much less produced with harmony, even by Nature herself."[87]

From even a small rise, the effect of a sunset upon the western landscape is to first make distinct and then to obscure the features of the land. This progression from light to dark at first delineates natural features with great precision. The sun's oblique rays emphasize the contours while the growing shadows spread from behind the ridges from east to west. Major Butler, in his ponderous fashion, attempted to capture for his audience what was essentially uncapturable:

Climbing to the top of this hill I beheld a view of extraordinary beauty. Over the sea of forest, from the dark green and light green ocean of tree-tops, the solid mountain mass lay piled against the east. Below my stand-point the first long reach of the cañon opened out; a grim fissure in the forest, in the depths of which the waters caught the reflection of the sun-lit skies above, glowing brightly between the walls of gloomy rock deep hidden beneath the level rays of the setting sun. I stood high above the cañon, high above the vast forest which stretched between me and the mountains; and the eye, as it wandered over the tranquil ocean upon whose waves the isles of light green shade lay gold-crested in the sunset, seemed to rest upon fresh intervals of beauty, until the solid ramparts rent and pinnacled, silent and impassive, caught and riveted its glance; as their snow-white, motionless fingers, carved in characters that ever last, the story of earth's loveliness upon the great blue dome of heaven.[88]

While the scenery may have been indescribable at times, these western travellers were usually willing to try, even while proclaiming the impossibility. Their efforts now prove valuable, for they documented the North American West during a period of great change; change that would in the coming years often make the land itself unrecognizable. Dams inundated peaceful valleys, mining wastes polluted lakes and rivers, and fences chopped the vastness into measurable units; while forests were cut to meet the insatiable appetite for timber. The few places that remain as they were over a hundred years ago can be quickly named and numbered.[89] In the illimitable West, we may have, at last, found the ultimate boundaries.

Mountains So Sublime

Anglo-American Attitudes

*English people are far more interested in American barbarism
than they are in American civilisation.*[1]

The social conflicts between class-conscious Britons and free-and-easy Americans were widespread, but not universal. W. A. Baillie-Grohman and Isabella Bird were just two among many travellers who mixed freely with nearly all classes during their western excursions. Like many British travellers, even those two accepting souls expressed surprise and amazement at American attitudes toward the immense and spectacular landscape of the West.

As a central fixture of the American belief system, the then-prevalent myth of expansion and domination was widely held and often expressed. The doctrine of Manifest Destiny promoted a particularly American exploitation of the West and its peoples. The so-called "free" western lands shaped American thought, politics, history, and relations with the Native Americans. The gulf between Britons and Americans was never wider than when the topic centred on the abuse of the land and the landscape, for the myth was not necessarily shared by these foreign travellers.[2]

The American Dominion

The exploitation, or "conquest," of the West drew considerable comment by British travellers. Yet, the Britons saw this activity as one having both positive and negative connotations. As sportsman W. A. Baillie-Grohman noted: "Mentally and physically, ethnographically and topographically the West is a land of experiment."[3] It was in the big country of the West where big men and big ideas had an opportunity to win big or lose big. Poet and mine supervisor James Thomson was willing to excuse some of this behaviour. "I think we must forgive the Americans a good deal of vulgarity and arrogance for some generations yet. They are intoxicated with their vast country and its vaster prospects."[4] The "intoxicated," as many now recognize, have great difficulty recognizing their rapidly diminishing capacities and increasing limitations. Baillie-Grohman was less forgiving; to him, American greed matched the mountains in scale:

Nothing on the face of the broad Earth is sacred to him. Nature presents herself as his slave. He digs and delves wherever he fancies; forests are there to be felled, or, if that process be too slow and laborious, to be set ablaze; mountains are made to be honeycombed by his drills and sluices; rocks and hills exist but to be blasted or to be spirited away by the powerful jet from the nozzle of his hydraulic tube. Landscape itself is not secure, for eminences may be levelled, lakes laid dry, and the watercourse of rivers may be turned off, as best suits his immediate desires.[5]

The apparent lack of limits among the West's vast vistas gave the westerner unbridled license to plunder and pillage the landscape. The American concept of private property, so alien to the Native Americans, encouraged this license. The owner of the property assumed a nearly absolute right to do whatever was wanted, no matter how destructive. As a corollary, property that was theoretically not owned, such as unclaimed government land, could be disturbed or destroyed with abandon. Travel writer Paul Fountain noted that by 1905, "nine-tenths of the game has been killed, nine-tenths of the trees destroyed, [which was] a sure sign of the immediate rise of a multitude of towns and cities, and human works of all descriptions."[6]

What's Mine is Mined

During mining booms and rushes, the miners cooperated to establish a method of recognizing "ownership" of specific sites. They also agreed on a way to acquire "title" to the water required to operate their claim. Their stakes were called "claims" because the actual title to the land was not always formally granted before the boom dissipated and the miners departed. In their search for productive ore, the miners moved mountains, rechanneled rivers, and destroyed forests. In the Colorado Rockies, as Isabella Bird noted:

[M]ining destroys and devastates, turning the earth inside out, making it hideous, and blighting every green

thing, as it usually blights man's heart and soul. There was mining everywhere along that grand road, with all its destruction and devastation, its digging, burrowing, gulching, and sluicing; and up all along the seemingly inaccessible heights were holes with their roofs log supported, in which solitary and patient men were selling their lives for treasure.[7]

On the border between British Columbia and what was to become Washington State, British surveyor Charles Wilson saw the transition as well. "The glen in which [the miners] were working was very pretty, but the natural beauties were fast fading under the influence of gold digging & the fine trees falling under the axe."[8] American miners following the gold rushes into British Columbia were, by their sheer numbers, usually credited with all of the social and environmental problems that ensued. In Colorado, poet James Thomson noted in his diary in 1872 that the hills "nearer Central [City were] all covered with large fir cones tho' scarcely a fir tree is now left … Near Central [where they are] skinned of their timber and torn & scarred with

mining, and rounded in low curves, the hills look new."[9]

Maurice Morris thought that Colorado's beauty exceeded the capacity of the miner to destroy it. Yet he was an eyewitness to one of the more insidious forms of destruction, the silting of streams from placer or hydraulic mining:

At last, as you approach the end of the ravine, the lovely valley of Idahoe, or "the gem of the mountains," as the Indians have well named it, breaks upon you with a beauty which man the ravager has been unable to efface, in spite of his wooden shanties erected in the fairest portion of the greensward, and the various appliances for

bar-mining which mar the smooth margin of the stream
running through it, making its crystal lymph as foul as
bilge-water …[10]

James Thomson also noted the effects of large
scale placer mining in a letter to his friend, W.
M. Rossetti: "The hills surrounding us have been
flayed of their grass and scalped of their timber;
and they are scarred and gashed and ulcerated all
over from past mining operations; so ferociously
does little man scratch at the breasts of his great
calm mother when he thinks that jewels are there
hidden. The streams running down the ravines,
or as they say here, the creeks running down the
gulches, are thick with pollution from the wash-
ing of dirt and ores."[11]

Morris and Thomson were among the few
British travellers who commented on the widespread pollution in the West. Although Britons
were gradually beginning to recognize the del-
eterious side effects of the Industrial Revolution
at home, it is not surprising that they seldom
mentioned it in their descriptions of the less
densely populated parts of America. In an aside

to his readers, William F. Butler wrote in 1873
that, "Britons can get on very well without
knowing much of any river, excepting perhaps
the Thames, a knowledge of which, until lately,
Londoners easily obtained by the simple process
of smelling."[12] It was as late as 1882 when Oscar
Wilde warned the citizens of Dayton, Ohio not
to let the factories pollute their city.[13] More typi-
cally, by 1892, Thomas Moran turned the Denver
smelter's plumes and particulates into a watercolour scene of picturesque beauty.[14] As most
travellers came to the mountains for a sublime
experience, it is not surprising that they chose
not to dwell on the unpleasant aspects.

TIMBER!

Forests were also at risk. In mining regions,
timber was either burned to remove it from the
land, or felled to provide lumber for tunnels or
flumes. Miners, of course, were not the only
ones to reconstruct the landscape for their own
needs. Paul Fountain wryly noted that, "all the

Mountains So Sublime

newly-born villages, towns, and cities cut their teeth on timber ..."[15] Sir Richard Burton contrasted the American attitude to forests with that of other regions he had visited:

A few trees, chiefly quaking asp, lingered near the station, but dead stumps were far more numerous than live trunks. In any other country their rare and precious shade would have endeared them to the whole settlement; here they were never safe when a log was wanted. The Western man is bred and perhaps born – I believe devoutly in transmitted and hereditary qualities – with an instinctive dislike to timber in general. He fells a tree as naturally as a bull-terrier worries a cat, and the admirable woodman's axe which he has invented only serves to whet his desire to try conclusions with every more venerable patriarch of the forest.[16]

Similarly, author Colon South was florid in his denunciation of those who despoiled his "charming views."

The mountain slopes were covered with picturesque clumps of brushwood, thickly interspersed with the huge, bleached stumps of trees, which, dotting the steep acclivities right away up to their summits, sometimes resembled a vast cemetery. At one period, the whole of these mountain ranges were covered with dense, primeval forests, and the scenery must have been superlatively magnificent; but the irrepressible and Vandalic hand of man, with man's exigencies, has penetrated the sacred recesses of Nature's sylvan temples and shorn them of all their original grandeur.[17]

He added that, "the time-honoured and aged monarchs of the forest quickly fell to the ringing axe of the lawless and unbridled invader. Picturesque and beautiful groves were soon levelled and laid bare, while silent, secluded nooks and dells were cleared out, and often became scenes of noisy and rancorous strife."[18] This was justified, as gold miner Frank Marryat expressed it, by the common feeling that, in California at least, "the supply [of redwood trees] is inexhaustible."[19] W. A. Baillie-Grohman, returning to interior British Columbia after a lengthy absence, lamented the changes that civilization had brought:

30. THE SALMON SEEMED INEXHAUSTIBLE WHEN THIS
PHOTOGRAPH WAS TAKEN.

A salmon run. William A. Baillie-Grohman. *Fifteen Years'
Sport and Life in the Hunting Grounds of Western America and
British Columbia* (1900). opp. p. 202. Courtesy University of
Idaho Library.

*To-day, alas! that charm has long vanished; prosperous
though dishevelled looking mining settlements line the
shores, the forests have suffered by great fires which, for
several summers, enveloped the whole country for five or
six months in dense smoke. Steamers filled with miners
and land speculators awaken the echoes by their shrill
whistles, which are answered by the yet more discordant
locomotive bell of several railway lines, and at night
electric light shows up the nakedness of the numerous
"towns" that have spring up on the shore, while the
surrounding mountains are over-run by indefatigable
prospectors in quest of silver-bearing galena veins, with
which these mountains are scored.*[20]

This is not to say that all Americans were guilty
of these sins. Some "civilized Americans,"
according to Richard Burton, "lament the
destructive mania,"[21] but the nature of the
wilderness and the American response to it was
more often than not one of exploitation and
destructiveness.[22]

The Game is Up

Collateral to the exploitation was an immense
amount of waste; the illimitable appearance of
the resources did not foster a regard for their
conservation. As novelist Catherine Hubback,
a niece of Jane Austen, acutely observed in a
letter from Oakland, California to her son in
Liverpool, "There's lots of talk & boast about the
size & power of this country, but that mostly is
only a phrase of self conceit."[23] Nowhere was this
more evident than in the slaughter of wild game,
particularly buffalo. Vast herds were annihilated;
many were shot for meat by professional hunters,

and many more were killed for less worthwhile purposes. Shooting game from the train at that time was as common as shooting road signs from pick-ups today. When antelope were sighted from Wallis Nash's train in 1877, "there was a perfect fusillade from the rifles and revolvers with which a good many of the passengers were armed."[24]

Baillie-Grohman also noticed this wastefulness; he remarked that, "the Western hunter seems to fancy the game resources of his home perfectly limitless, and exhibits a supreme indifference to the reverse side of the 'first come first served,' hence is often astonished at what he calls English squeamishness. To a friend a Western guide once said, 'You have come a good many thousand miles to shoot, and now that we have at last struck game where it is plenty, you shrink from depriving the rascally Redskins or a parcel of skin-hunters of what is just as much yours as theirs. Certainly you Britishers are strange chaps.'"[25]

Other "Britishers," no doubt as a function of their more communal island heritage, shared this

foreign sensitivity to the potential effect of their actions. In part, it came from a sense of British sportsmanship and "fair play," the qualities that made the Britons such promising targets for amusement, satire, and parody. But there was also an appreciation, apparently lacking among many Americans, for the conservation of the resources. John Turner-Turner, first a sportsman and later a professional trapper and hunter in the interior of British Columbia, observed his American counterparts in the field:

I remember one day striking the deserted camp of an American sportsman, who, marvelous to relate, had

torn himself away from his dollar collecting occupation,
to indulge apparently in an attempted extermination of
Wapiti. Close to his camp lay [the bodies of] eight cows
and calves. But perhaps I do this sportsman an injustice;
he may only have been getting his hand in preparatory
to purchasing a deer forest in Scotland, where his bags
could be reported to the world.[26]

To later travellers, the great buffalo hunts of
earlier days were the stuff of legend and myth.
Where once the buffalo covered the plains from
horizon to horizon, easily visible, and shot
from the trains without regard for the consequences, they quickly became but a memory. A.
B. Legard, writing privately to his family and
friends, noted that, "When the large herds are
crossing the track, it is not uncommon to have
to stop the train for them; and on these occasions
some people are so fond of wanton destruction
that they shoot them from the cars, leaving the
bodies to increase the already too plentiful signs
of the thoughtless destruction of these valuable
animals. Such, though, is the fate of all wild
game on this continent."[27] John Turner-Turner,

not much over a decade later was, like many passengers, still looking for wild game.

*On entering the wild and unsettled districts, I con-
stantly found myself peering into the distance in the
vain endeavor to discover the antelope, which are still
occasionally to be seen, though the vast herds of buffalo
frequently observed only a few years ago, have entirely
disappeared never more to cheer the heart of the hunter
en route to his hunting ground. I doubt if, from a train,
a single buffalo will ever be seen again, unless it be a
tame one accompanied by domestic cattle. These I have
seen and imagined to be wild until instructed to the
contrary.*[28]

The "hunt" had degenerated to slaughter, and the signs were left to rot on the ground throughout the West. Many, like Turner-Turner, reported seeing "hundreds and hundreds [of buffalo] observed at different times lying dead in every direction, in all stages of decomposition, some having been killed but a year before, many having been destroyed out of mere wantonness." He prophesied that in a "very few years hence, and except for perhaps one far distant herd and a few stragglers, the Buffalo will be extinct; it seems almost incredible that in so short a time, such vast numbers could have been slaughtered, but it is by no means a timid animal, and is easily approached, except in the now isolated condition in which it finds itself, where the wood is its only safety."[29]

It was not just that the buffalo were killed, but that there was no sport in their killing and a great deal of waste. This wastefulness extended to other game regions as well. Lord Dunraven stated that where "small parties of white men can travel through it without much risk, the game will very soon be driven off or exterminated. And what wonder, when they kill millions of buffalo for their hides, and thousands of deer and wapiti for their skins alone, leaving the bodies to rot and fester in the sun?"[30] Brother-in-law Arthur Vivian noted the change in Dunraven's Estes Park in Colorado, even by 1879: "Now, alas! things are different ... the game has been to great extent destroyed and driven off; and this last misfortune has been hastened by the habits of many American hunters, who delight in letting off at all distances and at anything they may chance to come across."[31] Lord Desborough, in planning his 1884 hunting trip, tried to discover "some great game resort in Canada such as Wyoming used to be not so very long ago before the buffalo and elk were killed down by meat hunters, hide hunters, and Indians." He was told "that no such place existed – there were elk scattered about in the Rocky Mountains, but [they were] much hunted by Indians ... The buffalo had disappeared as completely from British Columbia as they had from the states."[32]

Mountains So Sublime

One personal response to this extremity was so unsportsmanlike that the author, John Turner-Turner, felt obligated to offer an apology of sorts:

I know of a few places in America, and elsewhere, which have not yet been hunted, and where game is plentiful, and other localities from which they have not yet been exterminated, but when I recall to mind the disgraceful fact that three out of every five of the self-termed sportsmen who visit American hunting grounds are bent on slaughter, I refrain from making public these discoveries which have cost me so dear; rather than play into the hands of men like these, who I place on a level footing with the Indians, I must risk keeping a few true sportsmen out of their rights, for I think when one man discovers a good country he should make it known to his comrades in sport, who, if they are worthy of the term, will do little injury by selecting only good heads. Such as these are welcome to share my gleanings, and may rely on a prompt reply should they seek one from me, though a personal interview is more satisfactory. Let those who brag of killing big game by the dozen hold aloof; I have seen enough of their cruel and selfish work.[33]

By the end of the century, just keeping silent was not enough to safeguard the Rockies' hidden treasures. W. A. Baillie-Grohman, sitting in his Alpine *Schloss* filled with mounted trophy heads from many years of hunting, became an unabashed conservationist. He recognized that what was once inexhaustible had become limited. He understood that not only were the easy days of the hunt over, but also that a profound change had taken place in less than a lifetime:

In the days I am speaking of there was, as the reader will probably have gleaned for himself, no difficulty whatever about finding and shooting game, but rather to remember constantly the duty owed to prolific Nature of not killing more than one could make use of, and of thus wasting life merely for the sake of gratifying that deplorable lust of killing ... But of course in those days one had no idea that the extermination of big game would take place with such appalling rapidity. Tens of thousands were butchered for the sake of a few shillings obtained for the skin. [In addition,] railways, ranchmen, and miners have taken possession of what was once the sportsman's

*paradise. Many parts of Montana, Wyoming, and
Idaho are still worth visiting for the sake of sport, but the
old glory of those States is gone never to return.*[34]

Baillie-Grohman saw the imposition of game
laws by the fledgling territorial governments
as "the best possible proof, not only of the
mellowing effects of time, but also that there
is no frontier, no 'West,' left." And, myths of
the heroic West to the contrary, "to have to
acknowledge that the destruction of the bulk of
the big game there was the work of one single
generation is not a pleasant truth for the 'Makers
of the West.'"[35] Yet, recognizing that turnabout
was fair play, he added:

*American millionaires have for years past, it is well
known, ransacked the picture galleries of Europe,
where they garnered many of the masterpieces that
once adorned the walls of England's mansions or the
marble-flagged galleries of Continental palaces. Europe
has revenged itself by sending to the Western hunting
grounds her sportsmen, who have succeeded in capturing
there quite as many, and probably quite as irreplaceable,
chefs d'oeuvre, not of man's, but of Nature's choicest
handiwork.*[36]

This is but another way of stating that the real
masterpieces in North America are nature's, not
the fine art carried away from Europe.

A significant aspect of the eighteenth-century
Romantic Revolution, carried on through the
next century, was a rediscovery of "Nature,"
especially wild nature. In literature, art, and
drama, Native Americans were adopted as
nature's children. The "Noble Savage" was not
just at one with the wilderness, but provided a
sharp contrast to the ills of industrialized civilization.[37] Some visitors to the American West,

lumping them all into one stereotypical group-ing, saw the Native Americans as better "game preservers" than the whites. Comparing the pollution of civilization with the clean air and water of the West, Lord Dunraven, among many others, thought the "untutored" tribesman perhaps had the better idea.[38]

Others, such as John Turner-Turner, asserted just the opposite. He grouped Native Americans with all of the other Americans; "Indians are wanton destroyers of game, fully under the impression that the supply is inexhaustible, ever gratifying the desire of the moment regardless of consequences. Bitterly have many tribes already suffered, hastening their own starvation by reckless slaughter, failing to recognize that what in former days proved abundance for them, could not also supply the gradually encroaching white man, with the result that they have to an alarming extent been the means of their own destruction. I have never known an Indian lose an opportunity of killing any animal or bird, young or old, in or out of season …"[39] This

sentiment was also expressed by former Army "Serjeant" and later Indian agent in Washington Territory, R. M. Rylatt.[40] Yet, Turner-Turner also recognized that the Native Americans were not solely at fault.

Where are the vast herds of buffalo which existed but a short time ago, and what means my constantly having found their carcasses with hides, heads, and flesh intact? Was it that buffalo, being so easily approached, were constantly shot down simply for the gratification of seeing them fall; or was it the result of wild and reck-less shooting? Who were the wanton destroyers of these noble beasts? Not Indians I take it, or the extermination would have resulted long before.[41]

If it was not the Native Americans, then it must be the Americans. This more widely held sentiment was expressed by A. B. Legard:

The ever-shoving Yankee comes pressing on, self and the present time his only thought, and his only sentiment, "The d – l take the hindermost." In years to come people will suffer for the improvidence of the present generation. Men of sense see these things, and many laws are passed, and more being brought forward, to try to put some check to them, but without as yet the slightest avail.[42]

Even Rudyard Kipling expressed amazement at the sheer capacity of the Americans to take and take from nature. His prediction of an end to the ongoing deforestation has not yet been realized:

Also the great American nation, which individually never shuts a door behind its noble self, very seldom attempts to put back anything that it has taken from Nature's shelves. It grabs all it can and moves on. But the moving-on is nearly finished and the grabbing must stop, and then the Federal Government will have to establish a Woods and Forests Department the like of which was never seen in the world before. And all the people who have been accustomed to hack, mangle, and burn timber as they please will object, with shots and protestations, to this infringement of their rights.[43]

To some, such as Army officer William Butler, American exploitation of the landscape was a constituent part of their domination of the continent. He sarcastically suggested that:

To civilize a new land is the easiest of tasks if we but set about it after the American model. Here is the recipe. Given a realm from which the red man has been banished, tricked, shot, or hunted out; from which the bison and elk have been chased; a lonely, tenantless land, with some great river flowing in long winding reaches silently through its vast plains and mountain gorges: here, then, is what you have to do.

Place on the river a steamboat of the rudest construction. Wherever the banks are easy of ascent, or where a smaller stream seeks the main river, build a drinking-house of rough-hewn logs; let the name of God be used only in blasphemy, and language be a medium for the conveyance of curses. Call a hill a "bluff," a valley a "gulch," a fire-fly a "lightning bug," a man "a cuss," three shanties a "city." Let every man chew when he isn't smoking, and spit when he isn't asleep; and then — when half a dozen persons have come to violent ends — when killing has literally become "no murder" — your new land will be thoroughly civilized.[44]

A Cambridge lecturer, Shane Leslie, visited the United States four times between 1911 and 1935. As the nephew of Wyoming rancher Moreton Frewen and family friend of Lord Dunraven, he heard first-hand accounts of their western experiences. From that vantage, he was able to look back some fifty years and then forward another fifty to provide a long-term perspective on America's forest resources.

"The tree question will soon become a grave one," wrote *Walt Whitman in the 'eighties. The waste of timber cannot be told in board feet. Three-eighths of the forest have gone and the rest is going before the second growth has any chance of reaching the original grandeur. The timber on the Pacific is expected to last fifty years and* après nous le deluge *or rather the dust-storm.*[45]

We are long past the end of Leslie's second fifty years, and are barely beginning to accept the truth of his predictions. That they bore such little fruit is a consequence of the traveller's role as an outsider; whose only assignment was to bring back a report, without serving as conscience.

Many British travellers would have agreed with Leslie that Americans, in their exploitation of the western landscape, were insensitive to the long-term consequences of their wastefulness. British surveying team member Charles Wilson, for instance, stopped in Astoria at the mouth of the Columbia around 1860 specifically to look at its famed giant fir tree. Of historic Astoria, an early fur-trade entrepôt, he wrote, "hardly anything of its former state remains, the Yankees having started a city there; the immense tree, so celebrated, has fallen, having been chopped down for a wager by two of these 'go ahead' people."[46]

British travellers were quick to notice the overly familiar way in which Americans responded to their landscape. Advertising placards and huckstering barkers were merely one manifestation of their disrespect. From the transcontinental railroad crossing Utah, traveller W. G. Marshall remarked: "The sublimity of Echo Cañon is considerably reduced in the estimation of the lover of the picturesque and beautiful by the conspicuous white-paint advertisements which are seen daubed up against the red sandstone precipices just in the most striking part of the whole gorge ... The most frequent are 'SOZODONT;' 'GARGLING OIL;' 'PLANTATION BITTERS;' and 'SALT LAKE HOUSE, SALT LAKE CITY, $1.50 to $2.00 p[e]r day.'"[47]

Another form of disrespect toward the land was witnessed in the naming of things. Naming rivers, mountains, and valleys was an important function that permitted communication, but naming also carries with it an element of control. In the mountainous West, naming often seemed an attempt to bring the natural grandeur down to a more human scale. Isabella Bird particularly noted the "Garden of the Gods, in which, were I a divinity, I certainly would not choose to dwell. Many places in this neighborhood are also vulgarized by grotesque names."[48] Often, the naming included classical elements; Kipling noted a basin that, "some learned hotel-keeper has christened Cleopatra's pitcher, or Mark Antony's whiskey-jug, or something equally poetical."[49] The era's need to attach European cultural monikers to American geographic features seemed to have few limits.

At the giant redwood grove in Mariposa, California, Arthur Vivian commented: "A wretched cockney-like habit prevails of labelling with fancy names these splendid growths, just as if they were show potatoes or turnips produced by some would-be famous manure. Nailed on to the grand old giants are flat white boards, on which are painted such names as 'Caroline,' 'Andrew Johnson,' 'The Fallen Monarch' (the last two have fallen), 'The Faithful Couple' (a tree which is split into two a short way up), &c. &c. Visiting cards are also often affixed, and names cut into the bark, still further disfiguring the grand old stems. Now that the grove is the property of the State and possesses regular custodians, it seems strange that this bad taste should be allowed to exercise itself. It certainly mars the enjoyment of nature's works to have miserable placards staring you in the face at every turn ..."[50] His calling it a "cockney-like habit" reflects the common English antagonism toward the American sense of equality, equating what were certainly upper-middle class American tourists with London's lower orders.

34. CALLING THIS DOWNED GIANT THE "FATHER OF THE FOREST" STRUCK SOME BRITISH TRAVELLERS AS A DIMINISHMENT OF ITS NATURAL SUBLIMITY.

The "Father of the Forest." C. E. Watkins Photo. [76853] W. G. Marshall. *Through America; or, Nine Months in the United States*. London, Sampson Low, 1881. p. 328. By permission of the British Library, #1041083.

Wanton Vandalism

American graffiti has a demonstrably long history. Various prominent landmarks on the Oregon Trail suffered greatly from this kind of desecration. At Independence Rock, Arthur Vivian noted that because it was "so directly on the main emigrant road, it has always been a well-known halting-place, and the base of the rock is literally covered with names and dates."[51] In the same way, the Sentinel Rocks in Idaho, according to John Mortimer Murphy, were "covered with the names of pioneers, their place of residence, and the date of their arrival at that locality. These autobiographies are printed with black axle-grease, and the writers being amateurs at the printing art, their work resembles hieroglyphics at a distance. The names of many a Smith and Brown are stamped so indelibly on this rocky parchment that nothing but its disintegration by the action of weather and time can erase them."[52] That we now revere these scarred rocks as historical monuments sends a conflicting message to those we try to stop from spraying their names on rocks, walls, park benches, forest signs, subway cars, and other modern canvases.

Nature, after all, could always be improved on by memorializing one's name upon it. Kipling watched young American ladies write their names in the bottoms of Yellowstone Park's shallow geyser pools. "Nature fixes the insult indelibly, and the after-years will learn that 'Hattie,' 'Sadie,' 'Mamie,' 'Sophie,' and so forth, have taken out their hairpins, and scrawled in the face of Old Faithful," he wrote.[53]

As Kipling noted, awe is evanescent. In this account of his depredation, he yielded to temptation and joined his American companions in disturbing the landscape:

Inspiration is fleeting, beauty is vain, and the power of the mind for wonder is limited. Though the shining hosts themselves had risen choiring from the bottom of the gorge they would not have prevented [us] from rolling stones down those stupendous rainbow-washed slides. Seventeen hundred feet of steepest pitch and rather more than seventeen hundred colors for log or boulder to whirl through! So we heaved things and saw them gather way and bound from white rock to red or yellow, dragging behind them torrents of color, till the noise of their descent ceased and they bounded a hundred yards clear at the last into the Yellowstone.[54]

Kipling may have tossed rocks down a ravine, but he does not admit to putting soap down the geysers to watch them erupt, although he apparently gave it some thought. And he does not ascribe that impulse to some defect in the American character, but rather to the broader human condition.[55]

Surveyor Charles Wilson noted the contrast at around 1860 at one boundary cairn where, in the midst of beauty, "we found tokens of previous visitors in the shape of sundry Anglo Saxon names engraved on the stones, to which truly English record we refrained from adding ours. The view from this point was very fine, precipices and peaks, glaciers and rocks all massed together in such a glorious way, that I cannot attempt to describe it."[56] Today, in the minds of some, had Wilson added his name, it would have increased the cairn's historical value.

Yellowstone Park is pre-eminent in the West. It has so many wonders that the imagination is overwhelmed; one becomes satiated and loses interest unless the spectacular follows the marvellous. "For miles we drove till [our guide] bade us alight and look at certain falls," Kipling wrote. "Wherefore we stepped out of that forest and nearly fell down a cliff which guarded a tumbled river and returned demanding fresh miracles. If the water had run up-hill, we should perhaps have taken more notice of it; but 'twas only a waterfall, and I really forget whether the water was warm or cold."[57] Kipling later adds, "Miracles pall when they arrive at the rate of twenty a day."[58] Perhaps as a consequence, he also noted the need to post soldiers to protect the wonders: "Only the actual curve of the cataract stands clear, and it is guarded by soldiers who patrol it with loaded six-shooters, in order that the tourist may not bring up fence-rails and sink them in a pool, or chip the fretted tracery of the formations with a geological hammer, or, walking where the crust is too thin, foolishly cook himself."[59]

Britons also decried another form of exploitation that was perpetrated by the always present "gang of [a]cute Yankee guides, touts, and that ilk."[60] Baillie-Grohman, Lord Dunraven, and S. N. Townshend were among those who were appalled at the desecration of natural wonders by posters and billboards. Lord Dunraven wrote: "Nothing is more revolting to our instincts, more disgraceful to our civilization, than the system of trafficking in the charms with which Nature is so beautifully endowed."[61] Not only was Niagara Falls disfigured by posters and signs,[62] but also Colorado's Front Range near Denver suffered the same treatment.[63]

Litter was another common problem. Lord Dunraven plaintively lamented the casual tour-ist litter befouling his romantic spots. He had, he said, "worshipped at the shrine of Nature in many a lovely spot, desecrated by the sandwich-papers, orange-peel, and broken bottles of former devotees..."[64] Hunters were, as a class, also guilty of leaving a trail of litter in the wilderness. In Wyoming, sportsman John Turner-Turner complained that his guide refused to leave the well-marked trail used by so many other groups. "Nothing would induce [him] to diverge from the regular trail, along which year after year, hunters have been accustomed to escort their parties, and which from the amount of tins lying about would convey the impression that a personally conducted party of Cook's tourists had gone before."[65] Such mounds of slowly rusting cans are still evident in unexpected corners of the wilderness. American travel writer A. A. Hayes was obliquely sarcastic about their ubiquitousness:

But for one thing how shall they ... answer [for] the strewing of the whole country with the great North American tin can? From the Wyoming line to the

Veta Pass, from the White River Agency far out on the plains, lie terrible deposits, daily increasing, and rivalling gold and silver, in extent if not in value, of the whilom receptacles of egg-plums (whatever they may be), tomatoes, and succotash.

"Do you not think," gently asked a clever friend of the writer, as they drove past one of these shining piles, "that when the New Zealander is quarrying out the remnants of our civilization, he will come to the conclusion that the tin can contrasts unfavorably with the pottery of Etruria?"[66]

Appreciative Attitudes

This is not to say that the British travellers found the Americans completely insensitive to the glories of western scenery, but there was a paradoxical ambivalence about it. Francis Francis copied down this dialect expression: "Wal, sir, I tell you that that thar Yellowstone Park and them geysers is jest indescribable – that's what they are, sure!" and ascribed it to "all the packers, teamsters, and prospectors whom we consulted on the subject."[67] Kipling quoted several of the American tourists, mostly young women, each exclaiming that the scenery was "elegant."[68] And A. P. Vivian's guide was moved to exclaim, "Yes, sirree, quite a dig out, I guess," at Yosemite.[69] R. M. Rylatt, with a survey team in the British Columbia Rockies, expressed some amazement that even the packers found the views spectacular for, "they are not men likely to go into raptures at a pretty picture of natures[']...."[70]

Such an analysis of British characterization of the American response to the landscape is flawed, of course, because there would be little interest in agreement with their own attitudes; it is only when the Americans deviated from what was considered "right" that it was worth mentioning in a patronizing, humorous sort of way. Because Canada at this time was still a part of the British Empire, Canadian attitudes and activities did not deviate as much from the "norm." Sir Richard Burton expressed what was probably a common conception of American attitudes toward art and beauty: "It is true," he wrote, "that in America the class that can devote itself exclusively to the cultivation and the study of refinement and art is still, comparatively, small; that the care of politics, the culture of science, mechanical, and theoretic, and the pursuit of cash, have at present more to hold upon the national mind than what is disposed to consider the effeminating influences of the humanizing studies...."[71] The young ladies that Kipling encountered, uttering "elegant" over every geyser and canyon in Yellowstone Park, were merely expressing in their own idiom the same wonderment and awe that Kipling's sardonic tone fails completely to hide.

Travel writer Maurice O'Connor Morris, who observed pollution, and surveyor Charles Wilson, who regretted the loss of one of America's marvels to a bet, would have agreed that no matter what indignities – from litter to vandalism – that tourists placed upon the landscape, there was a sense that the western scenery was grand enough to take considerable abuse. Not that it, like the wildlife, could not be destroyed, but that man's lighter touch on the landscape was survivable. As John Bodley wrote of Banff before the advent of the strip mall, "even Canadian civilization, which has called this tract of country a 'National Park,' cannot vulgarize the Rockies, though the road from the station is dusty & lined with the everlasting electric wires."[72]

Today, this statement would be much more debatable. "Vulgarizing the Rockies," whether by destruction, disfigurement, or decimation of game, has been ongoing for over a century. The Rockies in their majesty still exist, but there are places where the beauty has been stolen. There are places where the forests will not return. There are places where the poisons are deep in the waters. Man's heavy hand has certainly touched the Rocky Mountains much more than the nineteenth century could ever have imagined.

7

Lost Landscapes

*Everything, in fact, belonging to America is on a scale of grandeur. Her rivers flowing
for thousands of miles through various climes, here reflecting the hardy pine in their
clear waters, and there sweeping through the regions of the cotton and sugar cane.
Her lakes, like inland seas, compared with which our most boasted lakes
are but as the ornamental ponds in a gentleman's park.*[1]

American character, we have been told, has been shaped by the vast open lands of the West.[2] From the Appalachians to the Pacific, rivers, mountains, notches and valleys, as topographical features and romantic illusions, have drawn the frontiersman and settler. Their experiences depicted in art and literature continue to provide images that shape the nation's discourse. That some of these images are erroneous and some are downright dangerous is a lesson that we consistently fail to learn.[3]

British character, on the other hand, has been molded by the island's watery boundaries. That an island nation's seafarers and soldiers could girdle the world with British institutions is but one of the surprises of their character. Today, we see Britain as if in decline and forget the character that contributed so much to the development of a North American culture or cultures. British travellers in the latter half of the nineteenth century were part of the crest of the imperial tide; the regression was still ahead.

At the turn of the twenty-first century, the still new lands of the West are made new again when seen through the insular, but not always provincial, eyes of the British travellers. Familiar places recounted by unfamiliar eyes are thus seen anew. We seldom know how accustomed we are to the familiar until the friendly stranger points out what we have been missing. Taking a visitor on a tour of one's own neighbourhood is always educational. Their unsuspecting questions often produce imprecise answers. The resulting appreciation for what was thought to be so well known tells us how much was unquestionably assumed.[4]

Travellers' tales are often of places we have never been, but their accounts are most interesting when we can compare their observations with our own. Time travel, viewed through the window of historic documents, produces travel accounts that are equally enlightening. Our memories are too short and our experiences are too limited to rely solely on ourselves. The observations of these time travellers provide comparisons and contrasts with our own experiences that serve to enlarge our own perceptions.

The British Traveller

Previous chapters introduced us to these travellers; from explorers to tourists, from hunters to sportsmen, from fops to financiers, from poets to miners. The story of their activities outside of North America has been slighted, but many were participants in the wider world outside England and beyond the Americas. Isabella Bird went on to write many more books of travel covering her journeys through the Middle East, Africa, and Asia. John Bodley departed America for a trip through South Africa; he lived out the remainder of his life in France. Lord Dunraven, in addition to being a journalist in North Africa, competed in international yacht races. Rudyard Kipling, of course, was a product of Anglo-Indian culture. Richard Burton's travels have become legendary. Catherine Hubback was a well-known novelist from a literary family. Clearly, these were not ordinary people.

Even the ordinary Briton, far from home, was something out of the ordinary. Meeting others from the homeland either brought comfort or embarrassment, but many travellers mentioned incidents with their compatriots. Both Rudyard Kipling and Isabella Bird took note of one common variety – the inflated English gentleman. Kipling called him "a young English idiot."[5] Bird particularly noted one, called "The Earl" by the Americans because of his "insular peculiarities."[6] Nearly as bad, to the rough-hewn Colorado pioneers, was an English doctor of "very extreme opinions." One American observer excoriated this "thick-skulled Englishman" for being "polished." Bird added, "To say a man is 'polished' here is to give him a very bad name."[7] Another, she recognized as "an English gentleman" given to play-acting.

This gentleman was lording it in true caricature fashion, with a Lord Dundreary drawl and a general execration of everything; while I sat in the chimney corner, speculating on the reason why so many of the upper class of my countrymen – 'High Toners,' as they are called out here – make themselves so ludicrously absurd. They neither

know how to hold their tongues or to carry their personal
pretensions. An American is nationally assumptive,
an Englishman personally so. He took no notice of me
till something passed which showed him I was English,
when his manner at once changed into courtesy, and
his drawl was shortened by half. He took pains to let
me know that he was an officer in the Guards, of good
family, on four months' leave, which he was spending in
slaying buffalo and elk, and also that he had a profound
contempt for everything American. I cannot think why
Englishmen put on these broad, mouthing tones, and
give so many personal details.[8]

There was, on both sides, between the Americans
in the wilderness and their British visitors, a lack
of appreciation for their similarities or differences. There was nothing compared to today's
attempts to welcome diversity. The British
traveller, in particular, was often patroniz-
ingly labelled, "eccentric." Being a newcomer
was often enough to be considered different, so
such tenderfeet provided much amusement. It
became a game on both sides to see who could

score points. Oscar Wilde won over the miners
of Leadville when he drank a cocktail without
flinching, for, he reported, "they unanimously
pronounced [me] in their grand simple way 'a
bully boy with no glass eye.'"[9] They were probably unaware that the six-foot-plus Wilde's gar-
gantuan appetite for food and drink had already
been demonstrated in San Francisco where he
had outlasted the local journalists in an evening
spent drinking.

S. N. Townshend certainly tried to underscore
the normality of the event in his story about
climbing Mount Del Norte in his carpet slippers.
It began innocuously enough. He went out after
breakfast for a stroll and a pipe. Behind the hotel
he found the ground, "gradually rising, I looked
round, and found I could see a little more by getting higher; at last I got so many hundred feet
that going back to change my slippers seemed a
folly." The scenery was bountiful and each height
of land led to another, each with more spectacular views. Back at the hotel he found it necessary
to assert that, "ascending this mountain in carpet

Mountains So Sublime

slippers was a feat, not an eccentricity, which latter uncharitable view is always taken abroad of an Englishman's conduct."[10]

Similarly, John Turner-Turner's nearly fatal, although wryly recounted, adventure in the wilds epitomizes the classic tenderfoot story of being lost in the vastness of the West:

I continued walking for hours, until I felt certain I must be nearly back at camp again, at length, failing to arrive, the disagreeable truth that I was lost began to dawn on me, but I journeyed on under the confident impression that our camp must be on the other side of the rocky ridge which I never lost sight of, I consulted my compass, but, only intending such a simple route, I had never taken my bearings at starting, and though it ultimately led me home, it was at that moment of but little service, however, knowing that a friend of mine was camped not fifty miles off, I felt rejoiced when I came across his footprints in the snow, these I determined to follow, and doubtless his hunter could put me in the right way, though how he was to know the direction of a camp which he had never seen did not occur to me, I diligently followed the tracts

[sic] for about two hours, when I came to a place where my friend had had an awkward slip, having narrowly escaped falling over a rock, I was at once struck by the remarkable similarity between his fall and one I had in the early morning, but as I closely examined the details, the faint suspicion which had framed itself in my mind became matured into positive certainty, namely that my friend was none other than myself, and that for the last two hours, I had been following on my own trail of the early morning.[11]

Some part of this eccentricity was what Major W. F. Butler called "that too true insularity which would be sublime." His example was the oft-told story of the British loss of the Oregon country, a vast domain claimed by both the United States and Great Britain between 1818 and 1846, because northwest salmon, unlike Scottish salmon, would not rise to a fly.

The commander of the "America" was fond of salmon fishing; the waters of the Oregon were said to be stocked with salmon: the fishing would be excellent. The mighty

"Ekewan," monarch of salmon, would fall a victim to flies, long famous on waters of Tweed or Tay. Alas! for the perverseness of Pacific salmon. No cunningly twisted hackle, no deftly turned wing of mallard, summer duck, or jungle cock, would tempt the blue and silver monsters of the Columbia or Cowlitz Rivers. In despair, his lordship reeled up his line, took to pieces his rod, and wrote in disgust to his brother (a prominent statesman of the day) that the whole country was a huge mistake; that even the salmon in its waters was a fish of no principle, refusing to bite, to nibble, or to rise. In fine, that the territory of Oregon, was not worthy of a second thought.[12]

As Butler noted by way of introduction, however, "stories widely told are not necessarily true ones,"[13] but this story was close enough to true that he used it to illustrate something about the British character. That the fly-fishing captain's denunciation of the whole Oregon country as worthless was commonly thought to have influenced the British treaty negotiations meant something to army officer Butler, who deplored the loss to British sovereignty.

Character is an issue only in so far as it provides some explanation for actions and their consequences. That part of British character that brought so many to the Rocky Mountain West in the nineteenth century may never be identified; more clearly visible are the currents that led them to explore, to visit, and to hunt in the West.

Opening of the West

The many accounts of British travellers in the Rocky Mountain West resulted from the confluence of American and British expansionism. As the West was opened up by railroad, an increasing number of British travellers, bored with the scenery of Europe and the Alps, came to the West to see what was new and different. The oddities and marvels of Yellowstone Park were but one extreme manifestation of the scenic riches of the American West. And the infrastructure to support such tourism developed very quickly, as quickly as the demand arose. One historian has called it the "tourists' frontier."[14]

In addition, there was a merging of interests, as both the Americans and the Canadians were completing their transcontinental transportation links during a period of British market expansion after the end of the Civil War. British support for the southern cotton markets had led to an estrangement with the ultimately successful northern capitalists. After the war, Britons found the West often more congenial, dominated as it was by expatriate southerners coexisting with the few northerners who had sought western gold rather than southern bullets.

Travel to the West was easier, as well. The mineral and agricultural booms, through gold rushes and homesteading, put great pressure on increased transportation. The completion of the U.S. transcontinental railroad in 1869 was arguably the most significant feature of a half-century of incredible expansion of trackage, far exceeding the rate of growth in Great Britain, France, and Germany. It was such an event, wrote Henry

M. Stanley, characteristically, that it caused, "the wilderness [to] be made glad."[15] The Canadian Pacific's completion in 1885 also demonstrated that steel rails and steam locomotives were engines of economic growth.

Improvements in transportation brought not only travelling Britons, but all of the conveniences of the "Gilded Age." Isolated rural communities, where life was, according to Isabella Bird, "moral, hard, unloving, unlovely, unrelieved, unbeautified, [and] grinding,"[16] could begin to tap into the broader world of newspapers, mass-circulation magazines, and, by the end of the century, mail-order catalogues.

The availability of game, unfenced and running free, was another attraction, particularly to that class of wealthy sportsmen who pursued their quarry from continent to continent. This was not an idle pursuit, but one involving a concentration of efforts and resources. For instance, when John Turner-Turner and his wife, "L.," were dropped at the Tongue River in Wyoming to await their hunting guide, their camp gear entirely filled a buckboard.[17]

Fashionable and Unique

British travel narratives derived much of their terminology and values from the Romantic Movement's adoption of the concept of mountainous sublimity. These fashionable values were shared with the Americans, but carried perhaps more resonance in the British Isles. There was certainly a larger literary tradition in England to draw upon. Isabella Bird delved into this poetic tradition to quote and proclaim:

This is truly the "lodge in some vast wilderness" for which one often sighs when in the midst of "a bustle at once sordid and trivial." In spite of Dr. Johnson, these "monstrous protuberances" do "inflame the imagination and elevate the understanding." This scenery satisfies my soul. Now, the Rocky Mountains realize — nay, exceed — the dream of my childhood.[18]

No matter how sublime the landscape, however, not everyone shared a sense of its importance in the face of the world's other pressures. British travellers were frequently an elite group in their appreciation for western skies and western lands. Only a few of them had chosen to try to make a living off the land, and most expected to return to Britain at the end of their trip. This freedom to leave provided a freedom to appreciate. Free from extracting a living, unlike the settlers, the travellers were more conscious of the other values in what they beheld. And what they saw included the diminishment of the western landscape. As one historian noted, "a romantic love of the vanishing Wild West could be no more than a self-indulgent affectation beside the triumphant official cult of progress, which meant the conquest of the wilderness by farms and towns and cities."[19]

Proto-Conservationists

American wastefulness and British sportsmanship converged in the travellers' comments of support for what might almost be called a beginning conservation ethic in the West. Many of the travellers were sportsmen who were quick to notice the diminution of game.[20] The wastefulness and destruction were greatly evident to many British travellers, and figured prominently in their accounts. On the frontier, however, there was also the conflict between hunger and sportsmanship. Surveyor Charles Wilson noted his dilemma:

After this I dismounted & got the whole brood, killing one with my gun, two with stones & two with sticks; what would some of the English sportsmen say to this wholesale kind of butchery! I was almost ashamed of myself, but the inward man crying out that fresh grouse was better than stale bacon overcame any conscientious scruples I might have had as to this unorthodox manner of procuring game.[21]

Agricultural pursuits also threatened the wild lands. "Professor" Lincoln Vanderbilt, using words possibly borrowed from another, poetically described "a beautiful miniature valley that seems to nestle and hide itself from the world, as though, like some timid damsel, it feared its beauty would prove its destruction. Such has been its fate, for some unpoetical heathen has ploughed up its virgin bosom and planted it with beets and other dreadful vegetables." He, like Wilson, was conscious of the fact that, "there is little poetry in the heart when the stomach is empty."[22]

British sportsmanship was a fundamental aspect of the British character. It channelled repressed aggression into socially acceptable activities, while setting limits to that aggression. In T. H. White's acerbic and anachronistic dismissal: "it [all] stinks of Sport ... and the Done Thing and the Best People."[23] While some sportsmen were content to participate in the nineteenth century equivalent of today's helicopter hunting of staked game, others gladly met real wilderness hardships directly in their quest for trophies. The hardship they suffered, an element of that "self-mastery" so admired by the gentlemanly ideal, provides some of the most adventuresome reading among these travellers' tales.[24]

The Traveller's Contribution

The nature of travel narratives is of going away, having adventures, and returning to retell the story of those adventures. The retelling is, of course, a shaping of the narrative to suit the audience and its needs. This narrative structure leaves out of the equation any effect on the people and places visited.[25] Anthropologists once followed this approach in their ethnographic studies. They defined their activities as going to a "foreign" land to ask obscure questions about local customs and beliefs and returning to shape them into a narrative. Now, it is generally agreed that instead of coming in and taking away, ethnologists must contribute back to the community. This did not happen solely out of altruism or anthropological consciousness-raising, but out of direct action by the people studied, who refused to cooperate unless they were helped in return. In the same way, it is now time for the inhabitants of the great West to return to these historic accounts and see what can be learned from them.

If there is a "lost" Western landscape, a world changed beyond recognition over the last hundred years, can it be rediscovered? What has been lost, and what can clearly be recovered in these travellers' accounts, is a landscape in the second, if not first, flush of discovery and appreciation. If 1890 is the date of the closing of the West, a date fixed by the Census Bureau and celebrated in historian Frederick Jackson Turner's famous 1893 essay entitled, "The Significance of the Frontier in American History," it also marks the attainment of statehood by four of the western territories and the beginning of a quarter-century of population growth that heavily impacted the region.

If we could see the West as truly and as freshly as did these travellers, if we could recover something of Charles Wentworth Dilke's exhilaration in breathing the clean air of Denver,[26] we might be able to discern what has been lost. Perhaps we could learn to treasure it as it was and as it should be. We have not yet learned the lesson that these travellers unwittingly tried to teach us: that the

West is not too big to be destroyed; that incremental damage, like compound interest, becomes consequential over time; and that remediation is slower, more costly, and less efficacious than preservation.

There are some today who have recognized what we have lost, and what we are still in danger of losing.[27] There are organizations and individuals who seek to preserve what is left of the vanishing landscape. But the West is no longer big enough, wide enough, or tall enough to absorb all of the pressures for development, to maintain traditional but destructive lifestyles,[28] and to permit the sharing of wilderness camps by backpackers and RVers. The intrusion of technology, as dams, tramways, mines, motor vehicles, or chainsaws, both adds and subtracts. But the accounting seldom considers the value of, to use one overly romantic image, a wolf's howl on the mountaintop.

There is more to it than George Lawrence's modest wish: "At the very worst, I shall never regret these latest American wanderings; for they brought much worth remembering, even if – as just judges should decide – little worth recording."[29] His observations, coupled with the many other recordings of the North American West, only a fraction of which have been mentioned here, provide more than a "little worth recording." They set forth a nearly comprehensive record of the landscape as it was. For it is the recording that aids the remembering – our necessary remembering – of our lost landscape. Travel writer Paul Fountain, writing just after the turn of the century, remarked that, "the land can never again be known as I have known it: the past is a fleeting picture which I have endeavored to fix ere it fades away for ever."[30]

Notes

PREFACE

1 Paul Fountain, *The Eleven Eaglets of the West: Travels in California, Oregon, Washington, Idaho, Montana, Wyoming, Colorado, New Mexico, Arizona, Utah, and Nevada.* New York: E.P. Dutton, 1906.

2 Jonathan Raban, *Passage to Juneau: A Sea and its Meanings.* New York: Pantheon Books, 1999. p. 184. Raban has also noted that "Traveling Englishmen abroad [like Alice in Wonderland] tend to see the rest of the world as consisting largely of mad queens and talking rabbits and the rest." Quoted in Ben Yagoda's *The Sound on the Page.* New York: HarperResource, 2004. p. xxx.

3 According to my mother's note to me in an inscribed presentation copy of *Kitchener and Other Poems* (1917), Canadian novelist, "Poet of the Prairie," and Calgarian Robert J. C. Stead (1880–1959) was her grandmother's cousin.

4 Gail Nomura has argued that both the Spanish-American War of 1898 and the Boxer Rebellion in 1900 should be included in any discussion of western history. She notes that the boundaries of the U.S. West also encompass its Pacific and Asian territories. Gail M. Nomura, "Significant

lives: Asia and Asian Americans in the history of the U.S. West." *Western Historical Quarterly*, 25:1 (Spring 1994): 71.

5 Oscar Osburn Winther, "The British in Oregon Country: A Triptych View." *Pacific Northwest Quarterly*, 58:4 (October 1967): 179.

6 George Mikes, *How to be an Alien*. London: Wingate, 1946. p. 10.

7 Oscar Osburn Winther, "The British in Oregon Country: A Triptych View." 179.

8 The landscape's effect on the regional literature is also explored in George Venn's "Continuity in Northwest Literature," *Marking the Magic Circle*. Corvallis: Oregon State University Press, 1987. pp. 84–109.

9 Quoted by Lloyd Lewis and Henry Justin Smith, *Oscar Wilde Discovers America, 1882*. p. 342.

10 Francis Samuel Marryat, *Mountains and Molehills, or, Recollections of a Burnt Journal*, by Frank Marryat; with illustrations by the author. London: Longman, Brown, Green and Longmans, 1855. Time-Life Books (Classics of the Old West) 1982. p. v.

CHAPTER ONE   FIRST VIEW OF THE ROCKIES

1 S. Nugent Townshend, *Colorado: Its Agriculture, Stockfeeding, Scenery, and Shooting*. London: "The Field" Office, 1879, p. 2.

2 Earl Pomeroy, *In Search of the Golden West; The Tourist in Western America*. New York: Knopf, 1957, p. 88.

3 Rudyard Kipling, *American Notes: Rudyard Kipling's West*. New ed. Norman: University of Oklahoma Press, 1981, p. 125.

4 Susan Armitage, "Another lady's life in the Rocky Mountains," in Bonnie Frederick and Susan H. McLeod, ed. *Women and the Journey*. Pullman: Washington State University Press, 1993, p. 28. Isabella Bird's contemporary in the Colorado Rockies was Hester McClung, a maiden aunt from Ohio.

5 Henry Morton Stanley, *My Early Travels and Adventures in America and Asia*. p. 181.

6 Robert G. Athearn, *Westward the Briton*. New York: Scribner, 1953, p. xii.

7 Marjorie Hope Nicolson, *Mountain Gloom and Mountain Glory; The Development of the Aesthetics of the Infinite*. Ithaca, NY: Cornell University Press [1959]. See also Simon Schama's *Landscape and Memory*. New York: Knopf, 1995, pp. 411–62.

8 Simon Schama, *Landscape and Memory*. New York: Knopf, 1995, pp. 457–78.

9 Carlos A. Schwantes, *Railroad Signatures across the Pacific Northwest*. Seattle: University of Washington Press, 1993, p. 113; see also Anne Farrar Hyde, *An American Vision: Far Western Landscape and National Culture, 1820–1920*. New York: New York University Press, 1990, p. 54.

10 Rudyard Kipling, *American Notes: Rudyard Kipling's West*. p. 26.

11 William Francis Butler, *The Wild Northland, Being the Story of a Winter Journey, with Dogs, across Northern North*

America, New York: Allerton Book Co., 1922 [1873], p. 202.

12 William Francis Butler, *The Wild Northland, Being the Story of a Winter Journey, with Dogs, across Northern North America.* pp. 218–19.

13 George Monro Grant, *Ocean to Ocean; Sandford Fleming's Expedition through Canada in 1872 by the Rev. George M. Grant,* [n.p.] M. G. Hurtig, 1967 [1873], pp. 231–32.

14 Charles William Wilson, *Mapping the Frontier; Charles Wilson's Diary of the Survey of the 49th parallel, 1858–1862, while Secretary of the British Boundary Commission,* Edited and with an introduction by George F. G. Stanley. Toronto: Macmillan of Canada, [1970], pp. 156–57. For a summary of the Commission's travails, see Kathleen S. Weeks, "Monuments mark this boundary," *Canadian Geographical Journal,* 31 (September 1945): 120–33.

15 R. Byron Johnson, *Very Far West Indeed; A Few Rough Experiences on the North-West Pacific Coast,* 2nd ed. London: Sampson Low, Marston, Low, & Searle, 1872, pp. 99–100.

16 Stephen Fender, *Sea Changes: British Emigration & American Literature,* Cambridge [England]; New York: Cambridge University Press, 1992.

17 See catalogue at the end of Arthur Pendarves Vivian, *Wanderings in the Western Land. With Illustrations from Original Sketches by Mr. Albert Bierstadt and the Author,* London: Low, Marston, Searle & Rivington, 1879.

18 Henry Morton Stanley, *My Early Travels and Adventures in America and Asia.* p. 170.

19 Richard Francis Burton, *The City of the Saints, And Across the Rocky Mountains to California,* New York: Harper & Brothers, 1862, p. 153.

20 Richard Francis Burton, *The City of the Saints, And Across the Rocky Mountains to California.* p. 162. A "ghaut" is an Anglo-Indian word, related to gate, for mountain pass.

21 Charles Wentworth Dilke, *Greater Britain: A Record of Travel in English-Speaking Countries during 1866 and 1867,* London: Macmillan, 1868, v. 1, pp. 120–21.

22 Lincoln Vanderbilt, *The New and Wonderful Explorations of Professor Lincoln Vanderbilt, The Great American Traveler, in the Territories of Colorado, Arizona, & Utah ... including the Gorgeous Scenery of the Rocky Mountains and the Sierra Nevadas.* pp. 21–22.

23 *St. Louis Post-Dispatch,* February 26?, 1882, quoted in Lloyd Lewis and Henry Justin Smith, *Oscar Wilde Discovers America, 1882.* p. 205. Readers undoubtedly recognize the more recent version of this observation: the provincial view from New York City as presented by artist Saul Steinberg on the cover of *The New Yorker* (March 29, 1976).

24 William Henry Grenfell Desborough, Diary, 1884, America and Canada. Buckinghamshire Record Office Mss.D 86/2 [Sept. 12, 1888 leaf 9].

25 John E. C. Bodley, Diary, 1888. Bodleian Library. MSS. Eng.misc.e.461 leaf 28a-b.

26 George Alfred Lawrence, *Silverland,* London: Chapman & Hall, 1873, pp. 30–31.

27 Maurice O'Connor Morris, *Rambles in the Rocky Mountains: With a Visit to the Gold Fields of Colorado*, London: Smith, Elder & Co., 1864, p. 74.

28 S. Nugent Townshend, *Colorado: Its Agriculture, Stockfeeding, Scenery, and Shooting.* pp. 101–2.

29 Colon South, *Out West: Or, From London to Salt Lake City and Back*, London: Wyman & Sons, 1884, pp. 91–92.

30 Colon South, *Out West: Or, from London to Salt Lake City and Back.* pp. 94–95.

31 Isabella L. Bird, *A Lady's Life in the Rocky Mountains*, Norman: University of Oklahoma Press, 1960, p. 25.

32 F. Barham Zincke, *Last winter in the United States, Being Table-Talk Collected During a Tour through the Late Southern Confederation, the Far West, the Rocky Mountains &c*, London: John Murray, 1868, pp. 230–31.

33 Stephen Fender, *Plotting the Golden West: American Literature and the Rhetoric of the California Trail*, Cambridge [Cambridgeshire]: Cambridge University Press, 1981, p. 72.

34 Paul Kane, *Wanderings of an Artist among the Indians of North America, from Canada to Vancouver's island and Oregon, through the Hudson's Bay Company's Territory and Back Again.* Toronto: The Radisson Society of Canada, 1925, p. 102.

35 George Monro Grant, *Ocean to Ocean; Sandford Fleming's Expedition through Canada in 1872 by the Rev. George M. Grant.* pp. 236.

CHAPTER TWO   BRITISH TRAVELLERS AND THEIR BAGGAGE

1 A. B. Legard, *Colorado*, London: Chapman and Hall, 1872, p. 56.

2 Lee Olson, *Marmalade and Whiskey: British Remittance Men in the West*, Golden: Fulcrum, 1993.

3 Robert G. Athearn, *Westward the Briton*, New York: Scribner, 1953, p. 185.

4 For travels in America in addition to Athearn's *Westward the Briton*, see: Max Berger, *The British Traveller in America, 1836–1860*, New York: Columbia University Press, 1943; Robert A. Burchell, *British Travellers Report on the White Conquest of the Trans-Mississippi West 1865–1905*, London: British Library, 1993 (First annual lecture, the David and Mary Eccles Centre for American Studies, July 1993); John F. Davis, "Constructing the British View of the Great Plains," in *Images of the Plains: The Role of Human Nature in Settlement*; edited by Brian W. Blouet and Merlin P. Lawson, Lincoln: University of Nebraska Press, [1975] pp. 181–85; Paul Fussell, *Abroad: British Literary Travelling Between the Wars*, New York: Oxford University Press, 1980; Jane Louise Mesick, *The English Traveller in America, 1785–1835*, New York: Columbia University Press, 1922, Reprinted: St. Clair Shores, Mich.: Scholarly Press, 1970; Allan Nevins, *America through British Eyes*, [New ed. rev. and enl.] New York:

Oxford Univ. Press, 1948; Richard L. Rapson, *Britons View America: Travel Commentary, 1860–1935*, Seattle: University of Washington Press [1971]; Edwina Jo Snow, "British Travelers View the Saints, 1847- 1877," *Brigham Young University Studies*, 31(1991): 63–81; Jeanne Olson, *Writing the Wild West: Travel Narratives of the late Nineteenth Century Tourist*, PhD diss., Arizona State University, 1996. For accounts of other travels, see, for instance: *After Africa: Extracts from British Travel Accounts and Journals of the Seventeenth, Eighteenth, and Nineteenth Centuries Concerning the Slaves, their Manners, and Customs in the British West Indies*, introduced and edited by Roger D. Abrahams and John F. Szwed, New Haven: Yale University Press, 1983; Lloyd Eason Berry, *Rude & Barbarous Kingdom; Russia in the Accounts of Sixteenth-Century English Voyagers*, Edited by Lloyd E. Berry and Robert O. Crummey, Madison: University of Wisconsin Press, 1968; Henry Romilly Fedden, *English Travellers in the Near East*, London, New York: Published for the British Council by Longmans, Green [1958]; Ray William Frantz, *The English Traveller and the Movement Of Ideas, 1660–1732*, Lincoln: University of Nebraska Press, [1967]; James C. Simmons, *Passionate Pilgrims: English Travelers to the World of the Desert Arabs*, New York: W. Morrow, 1987. More recently, scholars have sought grander themes in travellers' tales. An excellent example is Jeremy Mouat's "Morley Roberts in the Western Avernus," *Pacific Northwest Quarterly* 93:1 (Winter 2001/2002): 26–36.

5 Charles William Wilson, *Mapping the Frontier; Charles Wilson's Diary of the Survey of the 49th parallel, 1858–1862, while Secretary of the British Boundary Commission*, Edited and with an introduction by George F. G. Stanley, Toronto: Macmillan of Canada, [1970]; John Keast Lord, *The Naturalist in Vancouver Island and British Columbia*, London: R. Bentley, 1866.

6 Richard C. Mayne, "Report on a Journey in British Columbia in the Districts Bordering on the Thompson, Fraser, and Harrison Rivers," *Journal of the Royal Geographical Society*, 31 (1861): 213–23; H. Spencer Palmer, "Report on the Harrison and Lilloet Route, From the Junction of the Fraser and Harrison Rivers to the Junction of the Fraser and Kayosch Rivers, with Notes on the Country Beyond, as far as Fountain," *Journal of the Royal Geographical Society*, 31 (1861): 224–36. Mayne was also the author of *Four Years in British Columbia and Vancouver Island*, London: J. Murray, 1862.

7 Alfred P. Waddington, "On the Geography and Mountain Passes of British Columbia in Connection with an Overland Route," *Journal of the Royal Geographical Society*, 38 (1868): 126.

8 A. Waddington, "On the Geography and Mountain Passes of British Columbia in Connection with an Overland Route," *Journal of the Royal Geographical Society*, 38 (1868), p. 128.

9 George Monro Grant, *Ocean to Ocean; Sandford Fleming's Expedition through Canada in 1872, by the Rev. George M. Grant*.

10 R. M. Rylatt, *Surveying the Canadian Pacific: Memoir of a Railroad Pioneer*, Salt Lake City: University of Utah Press, 1991.

11 William Francis Butler, *The Great Lone Land: A Narrative of Travel and Adventure in the North-West of America*, 15th and cheaper ed., London: Sampson, Low, Marston & Co. [1872] 1891.

12 William Francis Butler, *The Wild Northland, Being the Story of a Winter Journey, with Dogs, across Northern North America*.

13 William Francis Butler, *Sir William Butler, An Autobiography*, London: Constable and Company, 1911.

14 Wallis Nash, *Oregon: There and Back in 1877*, London: Macmillan and Co., 1878; Wallis Nash, *Two Years in Oregon*, New York: D. Appleton and Company, 1882.

15 Colon South, *Out West: Or, From London to Salt Lake City and Back*. p. 156.

16 Clark C. Spence, *British Investments and the American Mining Frontier, 1860–1901*, Ithaca, NY: Published for the American Historical Association, Cornell University Press, [1958] p. 15.

17 George Alfred Lawrence, *Silverland*, London: Chapman & Hall, 1873.

18 James Thomson, Diary, May 18–Dec. 12, 1872. Bodleian Library, Oxford. Ms.Don.e.46; Notebook, 1872. Bodleian Library, Oxford. MS.Don.e.47. The other Thomson (1700–1748) published his most famous work in 1730.

19 A. B. Legard, *Colorado*. p. 136; 141.

20 Isabella L. Bird, *A Lady's Life in the Rocky Mountains*. p. 54; Earl Pomeroy, *In Search of the Golden West; The Tourist in Western America*, New York: Knopf, 1957.

21 Isabella L. Bird, *A Lady's Life in the Rocky Mountains*. p. 3.

22 Isabella L. Bird, *A Lady's Life in the Rocky Mountains*. p. 241.

23 Carlos A. Schwantes, *Railroad Signatures across the Pacific Northwest*, Seattle: University of Washington Press, 1993.

24 John E. C. Bodley, Diary, 1888. Bodleian Library, Oxford. MSS.Eng.misc.e.461. leaf 31b, leaf 32a. Biographer Shane Leslie erroneously transcribes "Chilliwack" as "Illicilli." *Memoir of John Edward Courtenay Bodley*, London: J. Cape, 1930, p. 199.

25 Rudyard Kipling, *American Notes: Rudyard Kipling's West*. p. 55. Exaggerating to make his point, Kipling added about 2,500 feet to Mount Hood's summit.

26 Rudyard Kipling, *American Notes: Rudyard Kipling's West*. p. 76.

27 Rudyrd Kipling, *American Notes: Rudyard Kipling's West*. pp. 86–87, 89.

28 Anne Farrar Hyde, *An American Vision: Far Western Landscape and National Culture, 1820–1920*. New York: New York University Press, 1990, p. 18.

29 Charles Russell, *Diary of a Visit to the United States of America in the Year 1883*, New York: United States Catholic Historical Society, 1910, p. 79, pp. 123–39.

30 F. Barham Zincke, *Last Winter in the United States, Being Table-Talk Collected during a Tour through the Late Southern Confederation, the Far West, the Rocky Mountains &c.* p. 234.

31 See also Greg Gillespie, "'I was well pleased with our sport among the buffalo': Big-Game Hunters, Travel Writing, and Cultural Imperialism in the British North American West, 1847–72." *Canadian Historical Review*, 83:4 (December 2002): 555–84.

32 Rudyard. Kipling, *American Notes: Rudyard Kipling's West.* p. 83.

33 Quoted in L. Milton Woods, *British Gentlemen in the Wild West: The Era of the Intensely English Cowboy*, New York: Free Press; London: Collier Macmillan, 1989, p. 39.

34 Patrick A. Dunae, *Gentlemen Emigrants: From the British Public Schools to the Canadian Frontier*, Vancouver, B.C.: Douglas & McIntyre, 1981, p. 121.

35 William Adolph Baillie-Grohman, *Camps in the Rockies. Being a Narrative of Life on the Frontier, and Sport in the Rocky Mountains, with an Account of the Cattle Ranches of the West*, New York: C. Scribner's Sons, 1882, pp. 9–10.

36 J. S. Campion, *On the Frontier*, London 1878. p. 76, as quoted by John I. Merritt, *Baronets and Buffalo: the British Sportsman in the American West, 1833–1881*, Missoula, Mont.: Mountain Press Pub. Co., 1985, pp. 111–12; Frank Marryat asserted that this was not true in earlier and less comfortable days: "They say we are a stiff and formal people: perhaps so; but in the mountains, an Englishman needs no further introduc- tion than to know a man for a countryman to place the best he has at the stranger's service." Francis Samuel Marryat, *Mountains and Molehills, or, Recollections of a Burnt Journal*, by London: Longman, Brown, Green and Longmans, 1855. Time-Life Books. (Classics of the Old West) 1982, p. 134.

37 Rudyard Kipling, *American Notes: Rudyard Kipling's West.* p. 107.

38 William Adolph Baillie-Grohman, *Fifteen Years' Sport and Life in the Hunting Grounds of Western America and British Columbia*, London: Horace Cox, 1900, pp. 4–5.

39 Park is a localism for mountain valley.

40 John I. Merritt, *Baronets and Buffalo: the British Sportsman in the American West, 1833–1881*, Missoula, Mont.: Mountain Press Pub. Co., 1985, p. 176.

41 Shane Leslie, *American Wonderland; Memories of Four Tours in the United States of America (1911–1935)*, London: M. Joseph, ltd., [1936] p. 251.

42 John Turner-Turner, *Three Years' Hunting and Trapping in America and the Great North-West*, London: Maclure & Co., 1888. Visit to Frewen's ranch, pp. 39–40; exchequer, p. 43. Turner-Turner dedicated his book on his American experiences to his wife, "L."

43 Henry Morton Stanley, *My Early Travels and Adventures in America and Asia.* p. 178.

44 Henry Morton Stanley, *The Autobiography of Sir Henry Morton Stanley,...* Ed. by his wife, Dorothy Stanley. Boston, New York: Houghton Mifflin Company, 1909, p. 53.

45 Francis Francis, Jr.. (or, the younger). *Saddle and mocassin*, London: Chapman and Hall, 1887; S. Nugent Townshend, *Colorado: Its Agriculture, Stockfeeding, Scenery, and Shooting*. London: "The Field" Office, 1879; Charles Wentworth Dilke, *Greater Britain: A Record of Travel in English-Speaking Countries during 1866 and 1867*, London: Macmillan, 1868.

46 Richard Francis Burton, *The City of the Saints, And Across the Rocky Mountains to California*

47 Robert Louis Stevenson, *From Scotland to Silverado*, edited by James D. Hart. Cambridge: Belknap Press of Harvard University Press, 1966.

48 Lloyd Lewis and Henry Justin Smith, *Oscar Wilde Discovers America, 1882*, New York: B. Blom [1967, c1936].

49 Mark Twain and Charles Dudley Warner, *The Gilded Age; A Tale of Today*, Hartford: American Publishing Co., 1873. The ironic title obscured the novel's underlying theme of commercial charlatanism and greed.

CHAPTER THREE   LITERARY TRAVELLERS

1 James Thomson, "Religion in the Rocky Mountains" in *The Speedy Extinction of Evil and Misery; Selected Prose of James Thomson (B.V.)*, edited by William David Schaefer, Berkeley, University of California Press, 1967, p. 66. The vertebrae/backbone simile was widely used in describing the Rockies.

2 Lloyd Lewis and Henry Justin Smith, *Oscar Wilde Discovers America, 1882*. p. 319.

3 Bertram Dobell, "Memoir," in James Thomson, *City of Dreadful Night*, London: Reeves & Turner, 1895, v. 1 p. lviii.

4 Rudyard Kipling, *American Notes: Rudyard Kipling's West*. p. 15.

5 Even as late as 1946, Kipling's tone still rankled; see James Eckman, The British Traveler in America, 1875–1920, PhD diss., Georgetown University, 1946, p. 339. Background is primarily drawn from Arrell Morgan Gibson's introduction to *American Notes: Rudyard Kipling's West*, New ed., Norman: University of Oklahoma Press, 1981; Martin Seymour-Smith's *Rudyard Kipling*, New York: St. Martin's Press, 1989 [1990]; and D. H. Stewart's introduction to *Kipling's America: Travel Letters, 1889–1895*, Greensboro: ELT Press, 2003.

6 Rudyard Kipling, *American Notes: Rudyard Kipling's West*. p. 48. Gambler Jack Hamlin, a recurring character in Bret Harte's tales of the California gold rush country, was based on the exploits of Henry J. "Cherokee Bob" Talbot, whose move from California to Idaho ended in a gunfight at age 29. See Herman Wiley Ronnenberg's "Cherokee Bob's Grave: The Historical and Literary Legacy from Fabulous Florence." *Echoes of the Past*, 1:6 (September 2004): 5–15.

7 Rudyard Kipling, *American Notes: Rudyard Kipling's West*. pp. 54, 55. The effusion was for Bridal Veil Falls.

Kipling noted: "'Bridal Veil,' jerked out the purser. 'D – n that purser and the people who christened her! Why didn't they call her Mechlin lace Falls at fifty dollars a yard while they were at it?' said California. And I agreed with him. There are many 'bridal veil' falls in this country, but few, men say, lovelier than those that come down to the Columbia River." p. 55.

8 Rudyard Kipling, *American Notes: Rudyard Kipling's West*. pp. 77, 55.

9 Rudyard Kipling, *American Notes: Rudyard Kipling's West*. p. 52.

10 Rudyard Kipling, *American Notes: Rudyard Kipling's West*. p. 65.

11 Rudyard Kipling, *American Notes: Rudyard Kipling's West*. p. 76.

12 Rudyard Kipling, *American Notes: Rudyard Kipling's West*. p. 77.

13 Rudyard Kipling, *American Notes: Rudyard Kipling's West*. pp. 86–87.

14 Rudyard Kipling, *American Notes: Rudyard Kipling's West*. p. 89.

15 Rudyard Kipling, *American Notes: Rudyard Kipling's West*. pp. 110–11.

16 Rudyard Kipling, *American Notes: Rudyard Kipling's West*. p. 117.

17 Rudyard Kipling, *American Notes: Rudyard Kipling's West*. p. 132.

18 Background is primarily drawn from James D. Hart's introduction to Robert Louis Stevenson, *From Scotland to Silverado*, Cambridge: Belknap Press of Harvard University Press, 1966; and from Ian Bell, *Dreams of Exile: Robert Louis Stevenson, A Biography*, New York: H. Holt, 1993.

19 Robert Louis Stevenson, *From Scotland to Silverado*. p. 127. This edition includes both *The Amateur Emigrant* and *The Silverado Squatters* as well as other writings from California.

20 Robert Louis Stevenson, *From Scotland to Silverado*. p. 143.

21 Robert Louis Stevenson, *From Scotland to Silverado*. p. 145.

22 Robert Louis Stevenson, *From Scotland to Silverado*. p. 146.

23 Robert Louis Stevenson, *From Scotland to Silverado*. p. 191.

24 Robert Louis Stevenson, *From Scotland to Silverado*. p. 199.

25 Robert Louis Stevenson, *From Scotland to Silverado*. pp. 251–52.

26 Hart, James D. Introduction, in Robert Louis Stevenson, *From Scotland to Silverado*. pp. xlviii–xlix.

27 Background information was derived from Lloyd Lewis and Henry Justin Smith, *Oscar Wilde Discovers America, 1882*, New York: B. Blom [1967, c1936]; and Richard Ellmann, *Oscar Wilde*, New York: Alfred A. Knopf, 1988.

28 W. F. Morse, in a letter to a Philadelphia booking agent, (1881) quoted by Richard Ellmann, *Oscar Wilde*, New York: Alfred A. Knopf, 1988. p. 152.

29 Wilde, Oscar, letter, April 17, 1882, to Mrs. Bernard Beere, in *The Letters of Oscar Wilde*, edited by Rupert Hart-Davis. New York: Harcourt, Brace & World, 1962. pp. 111–12.

30 Marshall Sprague, *A Gallery of Dudes*, Boston: Little, Brown, 1966. p. ix. As it happened, Sprague's gallery of dudes did not include Wilde.

31 Lloyd Lewis and Henry Justin Smith, *Oscar Wilde Discovers America, 1882*. p. 306.

32 Lloyd Lewis and Henry Justin Smith, *Oscar Wilde Discovers America, 1882*. p. 319, quoting Oscar Wilde.

33 Oscar Wilde, letter, 10? April 1882, to Helena Sickert, in *The Letters of Oscar Wilde*. p. 110.

34 Oscar Wilde, letter, April 25, 1882, to Helena Sickert, in *The Letters of Oscar Wilde*. p. 114.

35 Richard Ellmann, *Oscar Wilde*, New York: Alfred A. Knopf, 1988, p. 235, quoting Oscar Wilde.

36 Richard Ellmann, *Oscar Wilde*. p. 348, quoting Oscar Wilde.

37 Richard Ellmann, *Oscar Wilde*. p. 137n, quoting Oscar Wilde.

38 James Elisha Babb, letter, quoted by Richard Ellmann, *Oscar Wilde*. p. 192; "Babb, James Elisha," *National Cyclopedia of American Biography*, New York: James T. White & Co., 1937, v. 26, pp. 55–56.

39 Lloyd Lewis and Henry Justin Smith, *Oscar Wilde Discovers America, 1882*. p. 283, reproduces cartoon of June 10, 1882.

40 Richard Ellmann, *Oscar Wilde*. p. 239, quoting Oscar Wilde, "Impressions of America."

41 Oscar Wilde, "The American Invasion" (*Court and Society Review*, March 23, 1887) in *The First Collected Edition*, v. 15 *Miscellanies*. London: Dawsons of Pall Mall, 1969 [1908], pp. 77–78.

42 Oscar Wilde, letter, April 1885, to E. W. Godwin, in *The Letters of Oscar Wilde*. p. 174.

43 Oscar Wilde, letter, December 1898, to H. C. Pollitt, in *The Letters of Oscar Wilde*. p. 774.

44 Oscar Wilde, letter, March 27, 1882, to Norman Forbes-Robertson, in *The Letters of Oscar Wilde*. p. 109.

45 Background is primarily drawn from Henry M. Stanley, *The Autobiography of Sir Henry Morton Stanley*, Boston, New York: Houghton Mifflin Company, 1909; John Bierman, *Dark Safari: The Life Behind the Legend of Henry Morton Stanley*, New York: Knopf, 1990; and Douglas L. Wheeler, "Henry M. Stanley's letters to the Missouri Democrat," *Bulletin of the Missouri Historical Society*, (April 1961): 269–86.

46 Henry Morton Stanley, *My Early Travels and Adventures in America and Asia*. pp. 188–89.

47 Henry Morton Stanley, *My Early Travels and Adventures in America and Asia*. pp. 189.

48 Henry Morton Stanley, *My Early Travels and Adventures in America and Asia*. pp. 190. In a footnote, Stanley added, the prediction became true in less than the two years he had forecast.

49 Henry Morton Stanley, *My Early Travels and Adventures in America and Asia*. pp. 180–81.

50 Bierman, *Dark Safari*. pp. 40–42, Norman R. Bennett, *Stanley's Despatches to the New York Herald, 1871–1872*,

1874–1877. Boston: Boston University Press, 1970. pp. 408–415.

51 Henry Morton Stanley, *My Early Travels and Adventures in America and Asia*. p. 180.

52 Henry Morton Stanley, *My Early Travels and Adventures in America and Asia*. p. 178.

53 Henry Morton Stanley, *My Early Travels and Adventures in America and Asia*. p. 179.

54 Marshall Sprague, Introduction to Windham Thomas Wyndham-Quin, Earl of Dunraven, *The Great Divide; Travels in the Upper Yellowstone in the Summer of 1874*, Lincoln: University of Nebraska Press, 1967 [1876], p. vii.

55 John Bierman, *Dark Safari: The Life Behind the Legend of Henry Morton Stanley*, New York: Knopf, 1990, pp. 57–61.

56 John Bierman, *Dark Safari: The Life Behind the Legend of Henry Morton Stanley*. pp. 144–45.

57 Background is primarily drawn from Henry Stephens Salt, *The Life of James Thomson ("B. V."), with a Selection from his Letters and a Study of his Writings*. Port Washington, NY: Kennikat Press 1889 [1972]; Bertram Dobell's memoir in James Thomson, *City of Dreadful Night; Vane's Story; Weddah & Om-El-Bonain; Voice from the Nile; & Poetical Remains*, ed. by Bertram Dobell, with a memoir of the author. 2 v. London: Reeves & Turner, 1895; and William David Schaefer, *James Thomson, B.V.: Beyond "The City"*, Berkeley: University of California Press, 1965.

58 James Thomson, Notebook, 1872. Bodleian Library, Oxford. MS.DOn.e.47 "James Thomson's memorandum book relating to the affairs of the Champion Gold and Silver Mines Company, Colorado." [front endpaper]; Marjorie L. Reyburn, "James Thomson in Central City," *University of Colorado Studies, Series B, Studies in the Humanities*, 1:2 (June 1940): 196–97.

59 Bertram Dobell, Memoir, in James Thomson, *City of Dreadful Night; Vane's Story; Weddah & Om-El-Bonain; Voice from the Nile; & Poetical Remains*. p. lv.

60 Marjorie L. Reyburn, "James Thomson in Central City," *University of Colorado Studies, Series B, Studies in the Humanities*, 1:2 (June 1940): 193.

61 James Thomson, Diary, May 18–Dec. 12, 1872. May 23, 1872 [p. 6].

62 James Thomson, Diary, May 18–Dec. 12, 1872. June 14, 1872 [p. 21].

63 James Thomson, Diary, May 18–Dec. 12, 1872. June 14, 1872 [p. 21]. Biographer Salt transcribes "myself" as "my walk." Henry S. Salt, *The life of James Thomson ("B. V.")*, Port Washington, NY: Kennikat Press (1889) [1972]. p. 81.

64 James Thomson, letter, August 5, 1872, to W. M. Rossetti, quoted in Henry S. Salt, *The life of James Thomson ("B. V.")*. Port Washington, NY: Kennikat Press (1889) [1972], pp. 85.

65 James Thomson, letter, August 5, 1872, to W. M. Rossetti, quoted in Henry S. Salt, *The life of James Thomson ("B. V.")*. Port Washington, NY: Kennikat Press (1889) [1972], pp. 85–86.

66 Marjorie L. Reyburn, "James Thomson in Central City," *University of Colorado Studies, Series B, Studies in the Humanities*, 1:2 (June 1940) p. 201.

67 This view is supported by Marjorie L. Reyburn, "James Thomson in Central City," *University of Colorado Studies, Series B, Studies in the Humanities*, 1:2 (June 1940) see pp. 196, 199–201. Henry Paolucci's 1961 doctoral dissertation, published posthumously as a second edition in 2000, argues against this "biographical incubus" (*James Thomson's The City of Dreadful Night: a study of the cultural resources of its author and a reappraisal of the poem*. Wilmington: Griffon House for the Bagehot Council, 2000. p. 22.) Paolucci claims that Thomson's . muse was literary and "cultural" and not, as so many have believed, strictly biographical. This should not mean that Thomson did not rely, to some extent, on his observations and senses in constructing his poem.

68 Martin Smith-Seymour, *Rudyard Kipling*, New York: St. Martin's Press, 1989 [1990]. p. 58; 129; 187.

69 James Thomson quoted in Henry S. Salt, *The life of James Thomson ("B. V.")*. Port Washington, NY, Kennikat Press (1889) [1972], p. 109.

70 James Thomson, "City of Dreadful Night," in *The City of Dreadful Night; and Other Poems*. p. 7.

71 James Thomson, "City of Dreadful Night," in *The City of Dreadful Night; and Other Poems*. p. 17.

72 Marjorie L. Reyburn, "James Thomson in Central City," *University of Colorado Studies, Series B, Studies in the Humanities*, 1:2 (June 1940) p. 200.

73 James Thomson, "City of Dreadful Night," in *The City of Dreadful Night; and Other Poems*. p. 22.

74 James Thomson, "City of Dreadful Night," in *The City of Dreadful Night; and Other Poems*. p. 42; James Thomson, letter, August 5, 1872, to W. M. Rossetti, quoted in Henry S. Salt, *The life of James Thomson ("B. V.")*. Port Washington, NY, Kennikat Press (1889) [1972], p. 83.

75 James Thomson, "City of Dreadful Night," in *The City of Dreadful Night; and Other Poems*. p. 43.

76 James Thomson, " Insomnia (1882)," in *The City of Dreadful Night; and Other Poems*. p. 91.

77 Marjorie L. Reyburn, "James Thomson in Central City," *University of Colorado Studies, Series B, Studies in the Humanities*, 1:2 (June 1940) p. 185.

78 William David Schaefer, *James Thomson, B.V.: Beyond "The City"*, Berkeley: University of California Press, 1965, pp. 76–77.

CHAPTER FOUR THE POST–PICTURESQUE LANDSCAPE

1 John E. C. Bodley, Diary, 1888. Bodleian Library. MSS. ENG.misc.e.461. Oct. 3, 1888. leaf 33a.

2 Robert C. Bredeson, "Landscape Description in Nineteenth-Century American Travel Literature," *American Quarterly*, 20 (1968): 86. An alternative schema, one proposing more of a progression of modes,

can be found in I. S. MacLaren's The Influence of eighteenth century British landscape aesthetics on narrative
and pictorial responses to the British North American
North and West, 1769–1872. PhD diss., University of
Western Ontario, 1983.

3 Robert C. Bredeson, "Landscape Description in
Nineteenth-Century American Travel Literature,"
American Quarterly, 20 (1968), pp. 88, 94.

4 John F. Davis, "Constructing the British View of the
Great Plains." in *Images of the Plains: The Role of Human
Nature in Settlement*, edited by Brian W. Blouet and
Merlin P. Lawson, Lincoln: University of Nebraska
Press, [1975], p. 181.

5 Colon South, *Out West: or, From London to Salt Lake City
and Back*. p. viii.

6 Stephen Fender, *Plotting the Golden West: American
Literature and the Rhetoric of the California Trail*. p. 13.

7 Windham Thomas Wyndham-Quin Dunraven, *The
Great Divide: Travels in the Upper Yellowstone in the
Summer of 1874*, 2d ed. rev. London: Chatto and Windus,
1876, p. viii.

8 William Gilpin (1724–1804) wrote several books illus-
trating his theories; one of the most popular was *The
Wye and South Wales* (1782).

9 This discussion of the picturesque also draws from
Anne Farrar Hyde, *An American Vision: Far Western
Landscape and National Culture, 1820–1920*, New York:
New York University Press, 1990, pp. 14–23.

10 Robert Macfarlane, *Mountains of the Mind*, New York:
Pantheon, 2003, pp. 74–77.

11 Marjorie Hope Nicolson, *Mountain Gloom and Mountain
Glory; The Development of the Aesthetics of the Infinite*.
Ithaca, NY: Cornell University Press, [1959], p. 372, n.
2.

12 Douglas Cole and Maria Tippitt, "Pleasing Diversity
and Sublime Desolation: The 18th Century British
Perception of the Northwest Coast," *Pacific Northwest
Quarterly* 65 (1974): 7.

13 William Combe, *The First Tour of Dr. Syntax, In Search
of the Picturesque; A Poem*, Illustrated with eighty plates
by T. Rowlandson. Ninth edition with new plates.
London: Nattali & Bond, [1842].

14 William Combe, *The First Tour of Dr. Syntax, In Search
of the Picturesque; A Poem*, Illustrated with eighty plates
by T. Rowlandson. Ninth edition with new plates.
London: Nattali & Bond, [1842] p. 5.

15 Maurice O'Connor Morris, *Rambles in the Rocky
Mountains: With a Visit to the Gold Fields of Colorado*,
London: Smith, Elder & Co., 1864, p. 90.

16 Stephen Fender, *Plotting the Golden West: American
Literature and the Rhetoric of the California Trail*. p. 72.

17 Allayne Beaumont Legard, *Colorado*. p. 137.

18 William Adolph Baillie-Grohman, *Camps in the Rockies.
Being a Narrative of Life on the Frontier, and Sport in the
Rocky Mountains, With an Account of the Cattle Ranches of
the West*. p. 194.

19 Christopher Mulvey, *Anglo-American Landscapes: A
Study of Nineteenth-Century Anglo-American Travel
Literature*, Cambridge [Cambridgeshire]; New York:
Cambridge University Press, 1983, p. 13.

20 Arthur Pendarves Vivian, *Wanderings in the Western Land, With Illustrations from Original Sketches by Mr. Albert Bierstadt and the Author*, London: Low, Marston, Searle & Rivington, 1879, p. 373.

21 S. Nugent Townshend, *Colorado: Its Agriculture, Stockfeeding, Scenery, and Shooting.* p. 26.

22 I. S. MacLaren, The influence of Eighteenth Century British landscape aesthetics on narrative and pictorial responses to the British North American North and West, 1769–1872, PhD diss., University of Western Ontario, 1983, p. 639; 656–57.

23 John Keast Lord, *The Naturalist in Vancouver Island and British Columbia*, London: R. Bentley, 1866, v. 1, pp. 274–75. This view of Klamath Lake in Oregon was the result of Lord's horse-buying trip to San Francisco on behalf of the Commission.

24 George Alfred Lawrence, *Silverland.* pp. 65–66.

25 S. Nugent Townshend, *Colorado: Its Agriculture, Stockfeeding, Scenery, and Shooting.* pp. 88–89.

26 S. Nugent Townshend, *Colorado: Its Agriculture, Stockfeeding, Scenery, and Shooting.* p. 53.

27 S. Nugent Townshend, *Colorado: Its Agriculture, Stockfeeding, Scenery, and Shooting.* p. 24.

28 William Adolph Baillie-Grohman, *Camps in the Rockies. Being a Narrative of Life on the Frontier, and Sport in the Rocky Mountains, With an Account of the Cattle Ranches of the West.* pp. 114, 305.

29 Isabella L. Bird, *A Lady's Life in the Rocky Mountains.* pp. 166–67.

30 R. Byron Johnson, *Very Far West Indeed; A Few Rough Experiences on the North-West Pacific Coast.* pp. 243–44.

31 Isabella L. Bird, *A Lady's Life in the Rocky Mountains.* p. 190.

32 Maurice O'Connor Morris, *Rambles in the Rocky Mountains: With a Visit to the Gold Fields of Colorado*, London: Smith, Elder & Co., 1864, p. 129.

33 F. Barham Zincke, *Last Winter in the United States, Being Table-Talk Collected During a Tour through the Late Southern Confederation, the Far West, the Rocky Mountains &c.* pp. 230–31.

34 William Adolph Baillie-Grohman, *Camps in the Rockies. Being a Narrative of Life on the Frontier, and Sport in the Rocky Mountains, With an Account of the Cattle Ranches of the West.* pp. 228–29.

35 S. Nugent Townshend, *Colorado: Its Agriculture, Stockfeeding, Scenery, and Shooting.* p. 5.

36 Stephen Fender, *Sea Changes: British Emigration & American Literature.* pp. 296–97; Anne Farrar Hyde, *An American Vision: Far Western Landscape and National Culture, 1820–1920*, New York: New York University Press, 1990, p. 18; Christopher Mulvey, *Anglo-American Landscapes: A Study of Nineteenth-Century Anglo-American Travel Literature*, Cambridge [Cambridgeshire]; New York: Cambridge University Press, 1983, p. 13; Marjorie Hope Nicolson, *Mountain Gloom and Mountain Glory; The Development of the Aesthetics of the Infinite.* Ithaca, NY: Cornell University Press [1959], p. 143.

37 John Keast Lord, *The Naturalist in Vancouver Island and British Columbia*. p. 162.

38 John Keast Lord, *The Naturalist in Vancouver Island and British Columbia*. pp. 346–48.

39 William Adolph Baillie-Grohman, *Camps in the Rockies. Being a Narrative of Life on the Frontier, and Sport in the Rocky Mountains, With an Account of the Cattle Ranches of the West*. p. 209.

40 A. B. Legard, *Colorado*. p. 143.

41 Richard Burton, *The City of the Saints, And Across the Rocky Mountains to California*. p. 193.

42 John Keast Lord, *The Naturalist in Vancouver Island and British Columbia*. pp. 106–8. The "natural launder" refers to a trough, like a mining sluice.

43 Paul Kane, *Wanderings of an Artist among the Indians of North America, from Canada to Vancouver's Island and Oregon, through the Hudson's Bay Company's Territory and Back Again*. p. 191.

44 Paul Kane, *Paul Kane's Frontier; including Wanderings of an Artist among the Indians of North America*, edited with a biographical introduction and a catalogue raisonne by J. Russell Harper, Austin: Published for the Amon Carter Museum, Fort Worth, and the National Gallery of Canada by the University of Texas Press, [1971], p. 295.

45 William Adolph Baillie-Grohman, *Camps in the Rockies. Being a Narrative of Life on the Frontier, and Sport in the Rocky Mountains, With an Account of the Cattle Ranches of the West*. pp. 208–9.

46 William Adolph Baillie-Grohman, *Camps in the Rockies. Being a Narrative of Life on the Frontier, and Sport in the Rocky Mountains, With an Account of the Cattle Ranches of the West*. p. 77. Wapiti is an Anglicism for elk.

47 Stephen Fender, *Sea Changes: British Emigration & American Literature*, Cambridge [England]; New York: Cambridge University Press, 1992, p. 191.

48 Richard Burton, *The City of the Saints, And Across the Rocky Mountains to California*. p. 184.

49 John E. C. Bodley, Diary, 1888. Bodleian Library. MSS. ENG.misc.e.461. Oct. 1, 1888, leaf 31b.

50 Frederick Hawkins Piercy, *Route from Liverpool to Great Salt Lake Valley*, edited by Fawn M. Brodie, Cambridge: Belknap Press of Harvard University Press, 1962.

51 Hugh Honour, *The European Vision of America: A Special Exhibition to Honor the Bicentennial of the United States*, Cleveland: Cleveland Museum of Art; Kent, Ohio: distributed by Kent State University Press, 1975, p. 12.

52 George Monro Grant, *Ocean to Ocean; Sandford Fleming's Expedition through Canada in 1872*. pp. 240, 257.

53 George F. G. Stanley, Introduction to Charles William Wilson, *Mapping the Frontier; Charles Wilson's Diary of the Survey of the 49th Parallel, 1858–1862, while Secretary of the British Boundary Commission*. Edited and with an introduction by George F. G. Stanley. Toronto: Macmillan of Canada, [1970], p. 16.

54 Charles William Wilson, *Mapping the Frontier; Charles Wilson's Diary of the Survey of the 49th Parallel,*

1858–1862, while Secretary of the British Boundary Commission. p. 119. Stanley notes that Wilson's watercolours can be found in the, now, British Columbia Archives. p. x.

55 R. M. Rylatt, *Surveying the Canadian Pacific: Memoir of a Railroad Pioneer.* p. 113.

56 Wallis Nash, *Oregon: There and Back in 1877*, London: Macmillan and Co., 1878; reprinted: Corvallis, 1976. This claim is made in the reprint's jacket copy, which also confuses engravings with pen and ink sketches, but not in Kenneth Munford's biographical introduction.

57 Isabella L. Bird, *A Lady's Life in the Rocky Mountains.* p. 15.

58 Isabella L. Bird, *A Lady's Life in the Rocky Mountains.* p. 116.

59 Theodora Guest, *A Round Trip in North America, with Illustrations from the Author's Sketches*, London: Edward Stanford, 1895, p. 72.

60 James Carnegie, Earl of Southesk, *Saskatchewan and the Rocky Mountains: A Diary and Narrative of Travel, Sport, and Adventure during a Journey through the Hudson's Bay Company's Territories in 1859 and 1860*, Toronto: J. Campbell, 1875, p. 180.

61 William Francis Butler, *The Wild Northland, Being the Story of a Winter Journey, with Dogs, across Northern North America.* p. 9.

62 R. Byron Johnson, *Very Far West Indeed; A Few Rough Experiences on the North-West Pacific Coast.* p. 94.

63 Arthur Pendarves Vivian, *Wanderings in the Western Land, With Illustrations from Original Sketches by Mr. Albert Bierstadt and the Author.* pp. 238–39.

64 George Monro Grant, *Ocean to Ocean; Sandford Fleming's Expedition through Canada in 1872.* p. 91.

65 George Monro Grant, *Ocean to Ocean; Sandford Fleming's Expedition through Canada in 1872.* pp. 91–92.

66 George Monro Grant, *Ocean to Ocean; Sandford Fleming's Expedition through Canada in 1872.* p. 235.

67 Patricia Trenton and Peter H. Hassrick, *The Rocky Mountains: A Vision for Artists in the Nineteenth Century*, Norman: University of Oklahoma Press, 1983, pp. 262–63.

68 Charles Wentworth Dilke, *Greater Britain: A Record of Travel in English-Speaking Countries during 1866 and 1867.* p. 138.

69 For example, see illustration following p. 137 in Arthur Pendarves Vivian, *Wanderings in the Western Land. With Illustrations from Original Sketches by Mr. Albert Bierstadt and the Author*; see also Patricia Trenton and Peter H. Hassrick, *The Rocky Mountains: A Vision for Artists in the Nineteenth Century*, Norman: University of Oklahoma Press, 1983, pp. 116–49.

70 Arthur Pendarves Vivian, *Wanderings in the Western Land. With Illustrations from Original Sketches by Mr. Albert Bierstadt and the Author.* p. 418, 136.

71 George Monro Grant, *Ocean to Ocean; Sandford Fleming's Expedition through Canada in 1872.* p. 238.

72 Andrew Birrell, "Survey Photography in British Columbia, 1858–1900," *BC Studies*, 52 (Winter 1981–82): 51.

73 See, for instance, Weston J. Naef and James N. Wood, *Era of Exploration: The Rise of Landscape Photography in the American West, 1860–1885*, Buffalo: Albright-Knox Art Gallery, 1975.

74 Charles William Wilson, *Mapping the Frontier; Charles Wilson's Diary of the Survey of the 49th Parallel, 1858–1862, while Secretary of the British Boundary Commission*. p. 75. In spite of this statement, it seems the "official" Commission photographer was an unidentified sapper, specially trained for this purpose.

75 John Keast Lord, *The Naturalist in Vancouver Island and British Columbia*, London: R. Bentley, 1866, v. 1, front. For a selection of photographs by the British North American Boundary Commission from the Royal Engineer Corps Library, Chatham, Kent, see David Chance, "Balancing the Fur Trade at Fort Colville," *The Record* (Washington State University Library), 34 (1973): 22, 26, 35. Also see Robert D. Monroe, "The Earliest Pacific Northwest Indian Photograph (1860)," In *Three Classic American Photographs: Texts and Contexts*, ed. Mick Gidley, *American Arts Pamphlet No. 7*, Exeter: University of Exeter American Arts Documentation Centre, 1982, pp. 12–20.

76 Richard Burton, *The City of the Saints, And Across the Rocky Mountains to California*. pp. 185–86.

77 Oscar Wilde, quoted by Lloyd Lewis and Henry Justin Smith, *Oscar Wilde Discovers America, 1882*. p. 319.

78 Charles Russell, *Diary of a Visit to the United States of America in the Year 1883*. pp. 94–95.

79 Stephen Fender, *Plotting the Golden West: American Literature and the Rhetoric of the California Trail*, Cambridge [Cambridgeshire]: Cambridge University Press, 1981, p. 73.

80 Francis Francis, Jr. (or, the younger), *Saddle and Mocassin*. p. 24.

81 Francis Francis, Jr. (or, the younger), *Saddle and Mocassin*. pp. 13–14.

82 Charles William Wilson, *Mapping the Frontier; Charles Wilson's Diary of the Survey of the 49th Parallel, 1858–1862, while Secretary of the British Boundary Commission*. p. 123.

83 Charles William Wilson, *Mapping the Frontier; Charles Wilson's Diary of the Survey of the 49th Parallel, 1858–1862, while Secretary of the British Boundary Commission*. pp. 109–10.

84 William Francis Butler, *The Wild Northland, Being the Story of a Winter Journey, with Dogs, across Northern North America*. p. 268.

85 William Francis Butler, *The Wild Northland, Being the Story of a Winter Journey, with Dogs, across Northern North America*. pp. 241–43. For a contrasting view on Butler, see I. S. MacLaren, The Influence of Eighteenth Century British Landscape Aesthetics on Narrative and Pictorial Responses to the British North American

North and West, 1769–1872. PhD diss., University of
Western Ontario, 1983, p. 768.

86 Rudyard Kipling, *American Notes: Rudyard Kipling's
West*. pp. 110–11.

87 S. Nugent Townshend, *Colorado: Its Agriculture,
Stockfeeding, Scenery, and Shooting*. p. 113.

88 A contemporary translator might render this as "eye-
candy."

89 Arthur Pendarves Vivian, *Wanderings in the Western
Land, With Illustrations from Original Sketches by Mr.
Albert Bierstadt and the Author*. pp. 375–76.

90 Francis Francis, Jr. (or, the younger), *Saddle and
Mocassin*. pp. 117–18.

CHAPTER FIVE   "THIS SUBLIME CHAOS"

1 William Francis Butler, *The Wild Northland, Being the
Story of a Winter Journey, with Dogs, across Northern North
America*. p. 220.

2 William Adolph Baillie-Grohman, *Camps in the Rockies.
Being a Narrative of Life on the Frontier, and Sport in the
Rocky Mountains, With an Account of the Cattle Ranches of
the West*. p. 209.

3 Charles Russell, *Diary of a Visit to the United States of
America in the Year 1883*. p. 79.

4 Maurice O'Connor Morris, *Rambles in the Rocky
Mountains: With a Visit to the Gold Fields of Colorado*,
London: Smith, Elder & Co., 1864, p. 74.

5 George Monro Grant, *Ocean to Ocean; Sandford Fleming's
Expedition through Canada in 1872*. p. 232.

6 Rudyard Kipling, *American Notes: Rudyard Kipling's
West*. p. 86.

7 R. M. Rylatt, *Surveying the Canadian Pacific: Memoir of a
Railroad Pioneer*. pp. 100–101.

8 R. M. Rylatt, *Surveying the Canadian Pacific: Memoir of a
Railroad Pioneer*. p. 191.

9 William Francis Butler, *The Wild Northland, Being the
Story of a Winter Journey, with Dogs, across Northern North
America*. pp. 263–64.

10 Richard Burton, *The City of the Saints, And Across the
Rocky Mountains to California*. p. 153.

11 Richard Burton, *The City of the Saints, And Across the
Rocky Mountains to California*. p. 164.

12 Isabella L. Bird, *A Lady's Life in the Rocky Mountains*.
pp. 188–89.

13 A. B. Legard, *Colorado*. pp. 136–37.

14 William Adolph Baillie-Grohman, *Camps in the Rockies.
Being a Narrative of Life on the Frontier, and Sport in the
Rocky Mountains, With an Account of the Cattle Ranches
of the West*. p. 194.

15 S. Nugent Townshend, *Colorado: Its Agriculture,
Stockfeeding, Scenery, and Shooting*. pp. 17–18.

16 Isabella L. Bird, *A Lady's Life in the Rocky Mountains*.
pp. 93–94.

17 Isabella L. Bird, *A Lady's Life in the Rocky Mountains*.
pp. 166–67.

18 Arthur Pendarves Vivian, *Wanderings in the Western Land, With Illustrations from Original Sketches by Mr. Albert Bierstadt and the Author*. p. 229.

19 William Adolph Baillie-Grohman. *Fifteen Years' Sport and Life in the Hunting Grounds of Western America and British Columbia*. p. 2.

20 William Adolph Baillie-Grohman, *Camps in the Rockies. Being a Narrative of Life on the Frontier, and Sport in the Rocky Mountains, With an Account of the Cattle Ranches of the West*. p. 228.

21 William Adolph Baillie-Grohman, *Camps in the Rockies. Being a Narrative of Life on the Frontier, and Sport in the Rocky Mountains, With an Account of the Cattle Ranches of the West*. pp. 228–29.

22 Isabella L. Bird, *A Lady's Life in the Rocky Mountains*. p. 65.

23 George Monro Grant, *Ocean to Ocean; Sandford Fleming's Expedition through Canada in 1872*. pp. 236–37.

24 John Turner-Turner, *Three Years' Hunting and Trapping in America and the Great North-West*. p. 123.

25 John Turner-Turner, *Three Years' Hunting and Trapping in America and the Great North-West*. p. 57.

26 William Adolph Baillie-Grohman, *Camps in the Rockies. Being a Narrative of Life on the Frontier, and Sport in the Rocky Mountains, With an Account of the Cattle Ranches of the West*. pp. 50–51.

27 George Monro Grant, *Ocean to Ocean; Sandford Fleming's Expedition through Canada in 1872*. p. 232.

28 R. M. Rylatt, *Surveying the Canadian Pacific: Memoir of a Railroad Pioneer*. pp. 14–15.

29 R. M. Rylatt, *Surveying the Canadian Pacific: Memoir of a Railroad Pioneer*. pp. 14–15.

30 Isabella L. Bird, *A Lady's Life in the Rocky Mountains*. pp. 54–55.

31 William Adolph Baillie-Grohman, *Camps in the Rockies. Being a Narrative of Life on the Frontier, and Sport in the Rocky Mountains, With an Account of the Cattle Ranches of the West*. pp. 208–9.

32 Arthur Pendarves Vivian, *Wanderings in the Western Land, With Illustrations from Original Sketches by Mr. Albert Bierstadt and the Author*. pp. 136–37.

33 R. Byron Johnson, *Very Far West Indeed; A Few Rough Experiences on the North-West Pacific Coast*. pp. 243–44.

34 S. Nugent Townshend, *Colorado: Its Agriculture, Stockfeeding, Scenery, and Shooting*. p. 7. Rudyard Kipling was nearly flabbergasted by another tourist's assertion that he had an obligation to become a naturalized American citizen. Rudyard Kipling, *American Notes: Rudyard Kipling's West*, New ed., Norman: University of Oklahoma Press, 1981, p. 88. Dunraven had purchased his land, but was unsuccesfull in keeping out the homesteaders and other trespassers.

35 S. Nugent Townshend, *Colorado: Its Agriculture, Stockfeeding, Scenery, and Shooting*. p. 7.

36 Robert Louis Stevenson, *From Scotland to Silverado*. p. 128.

37 Robert Louis Stevenson, *From Scotland to Silverado.* p. 146.
38 George Alfred Lawrence, *Silverland.* pp. 65–66.
39 George Alfred Lawrence, *Silverland.* p. 33.
40 William Adolph Baillie-Grohman, *Camps in the Rockies. Being a Narrative of Life on the Frontier, and Sport in the Rocky Mountains, With an Account of the Cattle Ranches of the West.* p. 225.
41 Isabella L. Bird, *A Lady's Life in the Rocky Mountains.* pp. 54–55.
42 John Turner-Turner, *Three Years' Hunting and Trapping in America and the Great North-West.* p. 39.
43 Charles William Wilson, *Mapping the Frontier; Charles Wilson's Diary of the Survey of the 49th Parallel, 1858–1862, while Secretary of the British Boundary Commission.* p. 47.
44 Charles William Wilson, *Mapping the Frontier; Charles Wilson's Diary of the Survey of the 49th Parallel, 1858–1862, while Secretary of the British Boundary Commission.* p. 158.
45 A. B. Legard, *Colorado.* pp. 137–38.
46 George Monro Grant, *Ocean to Ocean; Sandford Fleming's Expedition through Canada in 1872.* p. 260.
47 William Francis Butler, *The Wild Northland, Being the Story of a Winter Journey, with Dogs, across Northern North America.* pp. 220–21.
48 John Turner-Turner, *Three Years' Hunting and Trapping in America and the Great North-West.* p. 163. L.'s diary, if it has survived to the present day, would be an interesting counterpoint to her husband's account.
49 John Turner-Turner, *Three Years' Hunting and Trapping in America and the Great North-West.* pp. 163–64.
50 John Turner-Turner, *Three Years' Hunting and Trapping in America and the Great North-West.* p. 164.
51 R. Byron Johnson, *Very Far West Indeed; A Few Rough Experiences on the North-West Pacific Coast.* p. 94.
52 R. Byron Johnson, *Very Far West Indeed; A Few Rough Experiences on the North-West Pacific Coast.* p. 99.
53 George Monro Grant, *Ocean to Ocean; Sandford Fleming's Expedition through Canada in 1872.* p. 291.
54 Richard Burton, *The City of the Saints, And Across the Rocky Mountains to California.* p. 31.
55 Arthur Pendarves Vivian, *Wanderings in the Western Land, With Illustrations from Original Sketches by Mr. Albert Bierstadt and the Author.* p. 263.
56 John Keast Lord, *The Naturalist in Vancouver Island and British Columbia.* pp. 104–5.
57 Charles William Wilson, *Mapping the Frontier; Charles Wilson's Diary of the Survey of the 49th Parallel, 1858–1862, while Secretary of the British Boundary Commission.* p. 103.
58 William Adolph Baillie-Grohman, *Camps in the Rockies. Being a Narrative of Life on the Frontier, and Sport in the Rocky Mountains, With an Account of the Cattle Ranches of the West.* pp. 41–42.
59 William Adolph Baillie-Grohman, *Fifteen years' sport and life in the hunting grounds of western America and British Columbia.* p. 109.
60 Francis Francis, Jr. (or, the younger), *Saddle and Mocassin.* p. 29.
61 Francis Francis, Jr. (or, the younger), *Saddle and Mocassin.* p. 13.

62 George Monro Grant, *Ocean to Ocean; Sandford Fleming's Expedition through Canada in 1872*. p. 235.

63 John Keast Lord, *The Naturalist in Vancouver Island and British Columbia*. pp. 190–91.

64 John Turner-Turner, *Three Years' Hunting and Trapping in America and the Great North-West*. p. 109.

65 Charles William Wilson, *Mapping the Frontier; Charles Wilson's Diary of the Survey of the 49th Parallel, 1858–1862, while Secretary of the British Boundary Commission*. p. 107.

66 Wallis Nash, *Oregon: there and back in 1877*. pp. 27–28.

67 Rudyard Kipling, *American Notes: Rudyard Kipling's West*. p. 55.

68 John Mortimer Murphy, *Rambles ...* p. 185. Today Shoshone Falls is not the spectacular cataract of before. Usually dry, its waters are pumped to the plains above for irrigation.

69 Henry Morton Stanley, *My Early Travels and Adventures in America and Asia*. p. 179.

70 John Keast Lord, *The Naturalist in Vancouver Island and British Columbia*. p. 107.

71 Maurice O'Connor Morris, *Rambles in the Rocky Mountains: with a visit to the gold fields of Colorado*, London: Smith, Elder & Co., 1864, p. 188.

72 Charles Russell, *Diary of a Visit to the United States of America in the Year 1883*. pp. 87–88.

73 Arthur Pendarves Vivian, *Wanderings in the Western Land, With Illustrations from Original Sketches by Mr. Albert Bierstadt and the Author*. p. 370.

74 George Monro Grant, *Ocean to Ocean; Sandford Fleming's Expedition through Canada in 1872*. p. 276.

75 Wallis Nash, *Oregon: there and back in 1877*. pp. 23–24.

76 Charles Wentworth Dilke, *Greater Britain: A Record of Travel in English-Speaking Countries during 1866 and 1867*. p. 141.

77 John Keast Lord, *The Naturalist in Vancouver Island and British Columbia*, London: R. Bentley, 1866, v. 1, p. 99.

78 George Monro Grant, *Ocean to Ocean; Sandford Fleming's Expedition through Canada in 1872*. pp. 139–40.

79 William Adolph Baillie-Grohman, *Camps in the Rockies. Being a Narrative of Life on the Frontier, and Sport in the Rocky Mountains, With an Account of the Cattle Ranches of the West*. p. 3.

80 Charles Wentworth Dilke, *Greater Britain: A Record of Travel in English-Speaking Countries during 1866 and 1867*. p. 121.

81 Francis Francis, Jr. (or, the younger), *Saddle and Mocassin*. pp. 12–13.

82 S. Nugent Townshend, *Colorado: Its Agriculture, Stockfeeding, Scenery, and Shooting*. p. 3.

83 George Monro Grant, *Ocean to Ocean; Sandford Fleming's Expedition through Canada in 1872*. p. 297.

84 Charles William Wilson, *Mapping the Frontier; Charles Wilson's Diary of the Survey of the 49th Parallel, 1858–1862, while Secretary of the British Boundary Commission*. p. 76.

85 Charles William Wilson, *Mapping the Frontier; Charles Wilson's Diary of the Survey of the 49th Parallel, 1858–1862, while Secretary of the British Boundary Commission*. p. 107.

86 Richard Burton, *The City of the Saints, And Across the Rocky Mountains to California*. p. 163.

87 Windham Thomas Wyndham-Quin Dunraven, *The Great Divide: Travels in the Upper Yellowstone in the Summer of 1874.* p. 173.

88 William Francis Butler, *The Wild Northland, Being the Story of a Winter Journey, with Dogs, across Northern North America.* pp. 277–78.

89 Michael Frome, *Battle for the Wilderness*, New York: Praeger, 1974, p. 23.

CHAPTER SIX ANGLO-AMERICAN ATTITUDES

1 Oscar Wilde, "The American Invasion" (*Court and Society Review*, March 23, 1887) reprinted in *The First Collected Edition, v. 15 Miscellanies*, London: Dawsons of Pall Mall, 1969 [1908], pp. 77–78.

2 To historian Robert G. Athearn, this enhanced their status as witnesses. Robert G. Athearn, *Westward the Briton.* New York: Scribner, 1953, p. xii.

3 William Adolph Baillie-Grohman, *Camps in the Rockies. Being a Narrative of Life on the Frontier, and Sport in the Rocky Mountains, With an Account of the Cattle Ranches of the West.* p. 20.

4 James Thomson, quoted by Bertram Dobell, in James Thomson, *City of Dreadful Night; Vane's Story; Weddah & Om-El-Bonain; Voice from the Nile; & Poetical Remains*, ed. by Bertram Dobell, with a memoir of the author. London: Reeves & Turner, 1895, v. 1, p. lv.

5 William Adolph Baillie-Grohman, *Camps in the Rockies. Being a Narrative of Life on the Frontier, and Sport in the Rocky Mountains, With an Account of the Cattle Ranches of the West.* p. 21.

6 Paul Fountain, *The Eleven Eaglets of the West*, New York: E.P. Dutton, 1906, p. x.

7 Isabella L. Bird, *A Lady's Life in the Rocky Mountains.* p. 193.

8 Charles William Wilson, *Mapping the Frontier; Charles Wilson's Diary of the Survey of the 49th Parallel, 1858–1862, while Secretary of the British Boundary Commission.* p. 125.

9 James Thomson, Diary, May 18–Dec. 12, 1872, May 23, 1872, [p. 6].

10 Maurice O'Connor Morris, *Rambles in the Rocky Mountains: With a Visit to the Gold Fields of Colorado*, London: Smith, Elder & Co., 1864, pp. 141–42. The invented name "Idahoe" or "Idaho," incorrectly considered of Indian origin, floated from Washington, D.C., to Colorado, to a steamboat on the Columbia, and then upriver to be attached to the territory split off from Washington in 1863. For a summary of this toponym's wanderings, see "Footnotes to history," *Idaho Yesterdays*, 8 (Spring 1964): 33–36.

11 James Thomson, letter, August 5, 1872, to W. M. Rossetti, quoted by Henry S. Salt, *The Life of James Thomson ("B. V.")*, Port Washington, NY: Kennikat Press (1889) 1972, pp. 84–85.

12 William Francis Butler, *The Wild Northland, Being the Story of a Winter Journey, with Dogs, across Northern North America.* p. 155.

13 *Dayton (OH) Daily Democrat*, May 2?, 1882; quoted by Lloyd Lewis and Henry Justin Smith, *Oscar Wilde Discovers America, 1882.* p. 342.

14 Reproduced in Patricia Trenton and Peter H. Hassrick, *The Rocky Mountains: A Vision for Artists in the Nineteenth Century*, Norman: University of Oklahoma Press, 1983, p. 204.

15 Paul Fountain, *The Eleven Eaglets of the West*, New York: E.P. Dutton, 1906, p. 125.

16 Richard Burton, *The City of the Saints, And Across the Rocky Mountains to California.* p. 170.

17 Colon South, *Out West: or, From London to Salt Lake City and Back.* pp. 134–35.

18 Colon South, *Out West: or, From London to Salt Lake City and Back.* pp. 135–36.

19 Francis Samuel Marryat, *Mountains and Molehills, or, Recollections of a Burnt Journal.* p. 110.

20 William Adolph Baillie-Grohman. *Fifteen Years' Sport and Life in the Hunting Grounds of Western America and British Columbia.* p. 109.

21 Richard Burton, *The City of the Saints, And Across the Rocky Mountains to California.* p. 170.

22 For a summary of more positive responses, see: Lee Clark Mitchell, *Witnesses to a Vanishing America: The Nineteenth-Century Response*, Princeton, Princeton University Press, c1981, pp. 54–63.

23 Catherine Hubback, Letters, Oakland, CA, 1871–1876, to son John and daughter-in-law Mary, Liverpool. Bodleian Library, Oxford. MS.Eng.lett.e.150 Letter to John, Sept. 23, 1872? Also see: Tamara S. Wagner's "Catherine Hubback (1818–1877): An Overview." http://www.victorianweb.org/authors/hubback.

24 Wallis Nash, *Oregon: there and back in 1877.* p. 24.

25 William Adolph Baillie-Grohman, *Camps in the Rockies. Being a Narrative of Life on the Frontier, and Sport in the Rocky Mountains, With an Account of the Cattle Ranches of the West.* p. 151.

26 John Turner-Turner, *Three Years' Hunting and Trapping in America and the Great North-West.* p. 167.

27 Allayne Beaumont Legard, *Colorado.* pp. 13–14.

28 John Turner-Turner, *Three Years' Hunting and Trapping in America and the Great North-West.* p. 19. In some parts of the West domestic cattle are referred to as "slow elk," a sardonic reference to both their usurpation of the range and their role as surrogate poacher targets.

29 John Turner-Turner, *Three Years' Hunting and Trapping in America and the Great North-West.* p. 35.

30 Windham Thomas Wyndham-Quin Dunraven, *The Great Divide: Travels in the Upper Yellowstone in the Summer of 1874.* p. 10.

31 Arthur Pendarves Vivian, *Wanderings in the Western Land, With Illustrations from Original Sketches by Mr. Albert Bierstadt and the Author.* pp. 140–41.

32 William Henry Grenfell Desborough, 1st Baron. Diary, 1884, America and Canada. MSS.D 86/2 Buckinghamshire Record Office, County Hall, Aylesbury, Nov. 9, 1884, [pp. 19–20].

33 John Turner-Turner, *Three Years' Hunting and Trapping in America and the Great North-West*. p. 167.

34 William Adolph Baillie-Grohman, *Fifteen years' sport and life in the hunting grounds of western America and British Columbia*. pp. 24, 26.

35 William Adolph Baillie-Grohman, *Fifteen years' sport and life in the hunting grounds of western America and British Columbia*. p. 28.

36 William Adolph Baillie-Grohman, *Fifteen years' sport and life in the hunting grounds of western America and British Columbia*. p. 43.

37 Patricia Nelson Limerick, *The Legacy of Conquest: The Unbroken Past of the American West*, New York: Norton, 1987, p. 215.

38 Windham Thomas Wyndham-Quin Dunraven, *The Great Divide: Travels in the Upper Yellowstone in the Summer of 1874*. p. 10.

39 John Turner-Turner, *Three Years' Hunting and Trapping in America and the Great North-West*. p. 168.

40 R. M. Rylatt, *Surveying the Canadian Pacific: Memoir of a Railroad Pioneer*. p. 165.

41 John Turner-Turner, *Three Years' Hunting and Trapping in America and the Great North-West*. p. 167.

42 Allayne Beaumont Legard, *Colorado*. pp. 13–14.

43 Rudyard Kipling, *American Notes: Rudyard Kipling's West*. p. 150.

44 William Francis Butler, *The Wild Northland, Being the Story of a Winter Journey, with Dogs, across Northern North America*. pp. 11–12.

45 Shane Leslie, *American Wonderland; Memories of Four Tours in the United States of America (1911–1935)*. p. 229.

46 Charles William Wilson, *Mapping the Frontier; Charles Wilson's Diary of the Survey of the 49th Parallel, 1858–1862, while Secretary of the British Boundary Commission*. pp. 89–90.

47 W. G. Marshall, *Through America: or, Nine Months in the United States*, London: Sampson Low, 1881, p. 143.

48 Isabella L. Bird, *A Lady's Life in the Rocky Mountains*. p. 156.

49 Rudyard Kipling, *American Notes: Rudyard Kipling's West*. pp. 89–90.

50 Arthur Pendarves Vivian, *Wanderings in the Western Land, With Illustrations from Original Sketches by Mr. Albert Bierstadt and the Author*. pp. 372–73.

51 Arthur Pendarves Vivian, *Wanderings in the Western Land, With Illustrations from Original Sketches by Mr. Albert Bierstadt and the Author*. p. 281. See also Frederick Hawkins Piercy, *Route from Liverpool to Great Salt Lake Valley*, edited by Fawn M. Brodie, Cambridge: Belknap Press of Harvard University Press, 1962, p. 122.

52 John Mortimer Murphy, *Rambles* ... p. 187.

53 Rudyard Kipling, *American Notes: Rudyard Kipling's West*. p. 104.

54 Rudyard Kipling, *American Notes: Rudyard Kipling's West*. pp. 110–11.

55 Rudyard Kipling, *American Notes: Rudyard Kipling's West*. p. 103; Carl Schreier, in his *Field Guide to*

Yellowstone's Geysers, Hot Springs and Fumaroles, Moose, Wyoming: Homestead Publishing, 1987, notes, by warning against it, that this is still a persistent problem. p. 6.

56 Charles William Wilson, *Mapping the Frontier; Charles Wilson's Diary of the Survey of the 49th Parallel, 1858–1862, while Secretary of the British Boundary Commission.* pp. 159–60.

57 Rudyard Kipling, *American Notes: Rudyard Kipling's West.* p. 97.

58 Rudyard Kipling, *American Notes: Rudyard Kipling's West.* p. 106.

59 Rudyard Kipling, *American Notes: Rudyard Kipling's West.* p. 90.

60 William Adolph Baillie-Grohman, *Camps in the Rockies. Being a Narrative of Life on the Frontier, and Sport in the Rocky Mountains, With an Account of the Cattle Ranches of the West.* p. 296.

61 Windham Thomas Wyndham-Quin Dunraven, *The Great Divide: Travels in the Upper Yellowstone in the Summer of 1874.* p. 18.

62 Arthur Pendarves Vivian, *Wanderings in the Western Land, With Illustrations from Original Sketches by Mr. Albert Bierstadt and the Author.* p. 373.

63 S. Nugent Townshend, *Colorado: Its Agriculture, Stockfeeding, Scenery, and Shooting.* p. 26.

64 Windham Thomas Wyndham-Quin Dunraven, *The Great Divide: Travels in the Upper Yellowstone in the Summer of 1874.* p. 16.

65 John Turner-Turner, *Three Years' Hunting and Trapping in America and the Great North-West.* p 26.

66 A. A. Hayes, *New Colorado and the Santa Fe Trail*, New York: Harper & Brothers, 1880, p. 125. Can dumps such as these are, as Hayes slyly suggests, a problem for today's historical archaeologists, although few of them are New Zealanders.

67 Francis Francis, Jr. (or, the younger), *Saddle and Mocassin.* p. 1.

68 Rudyard Kipling, *American Notes: Rudyard Kipling's West.* p. 86, 104.

69 Arthur Pendarves Vivian, *Wanderings in the Western Land, With Illustrations from Original Sketches by Mr. Albert Bierstadt and the Author.* p. 375.

70 R. M. Rylatt, *Surveying the Canadian Pacific: Memoir of a Railroad Pioneer.* p. 114.

71 Richard Burton, *The City of the Saints, And Across the Rocky Mountains to California.* p. 185.

72 John E. C. Bodley, Diary, 1888. Bodleian Library. MSS. ENG.misc.e.461, Sept. 30, 1888, leaf 29a.

CHAPTER SEVEN   LOST LANDSCAPES

1 S. J. Abington, *The "Great West"*, London: Educational Trading Company, 1871, pp. 5–6.

2 Roderick Nash, "Qualitative Landscape Values: The Historical Perspective." in *Landscape Assessment: Values, Perceptions, and Resources*, edited by Ervin H. Zube, Robert O. Brush, and Julius G. Fabos. Stroudsburg,

PA: Dowden, Hutchinson & Ross, 1975, pp. 11–13; Donald Worster ascribes it to a sense of "Eden restored." Donald Worster, *The Wealth of Nature*. New York: Oxford University Press, 1993, p. 10.

3 See, for instance: Anne F. Hyde, "Cultural Filters: The Significance of Perception in the History of the American West," *Western Historical Quarterly*, 25:3 (August 1993): 351–74. Belief in the myth led poacher Claude Dallas to kill two Idaho game officers in 1981 and a local jury to come within an inch of acquitting him. See Cort Conley, *Idaho Loners: Hermits, Solitaries, and Individualists*, Cambridge: Backeddy Books, 1994. pp. 201–62.

4 Patricia Nelson Limerick, "The shadows of heaven itself," in *Atlas of the New West: Portrait of a Changing Region*, New York: Norton, 1997, p. 171.

5 Rudyard Kipling, *American Notes: Rudyard Kipling's West*. p. 107.

6 Isabella L. Bird, *A Lady's Life in the Rocky Mountains*. p. 112.

7 Isabella L. Bird, *A Lady's Life in the Rocky Mountains*. pp. 50–51.

8 Isabella L. Bird, *A Lady's Life in the Rocky Mountains*. pp. 176–77.

9 Oscar Wilde, letter, April 17, 1882, to Mrs. Bernard Beere, in *The Letters of Oscar Wilde*. p. 112.

10 S. Nugent Townshend, *Colorado: Its Agriculture, Stockfeeding, Scenery, and Shooting*. pp. 17–18.

11 John Turner-Turner, *Three Years' Hunting and Trapping in America and the Great North-West*. pp. 32–33.

12 William Francis Butler, *The Wild Northland, Being the Story of a Winter Journey, with Dogs, across Northern North America*. pp. 317–18. Roderick Finlayson, then in charge of the HBC Fort Victoria, is apparently the source of this story, later — as by Butler — much embellished. The disappointed Captain's brother, the Earl of Aberdeen, was then Foreign Minister, later Prime Minister of England. See Roderick Finlayson, Biography (1891) http://collections.ic.gc.ca/salish/trad/rodfin.htm.

13 William Francis Butler, *The Wild Northland, Being the Story of a Winter Journey, with Dogs, across Northern North America*. p. 317.

14 Earl Pomeroy, *In Search of the Golden West; the Tourist in Western America*. p. 3.

15 Henry Morton Stanley, *My Early Travels and Adventures in America and Asia*. pp. 188–90.

16 Isabella L. Bird, *A Lady's Life in the Rocky Mountains*. p. 50.

17 John Turner-Turner, *Three Years' Hunting and Trapping in America and the Great North-West* pp. 19–20.

18 Isabella L. Bird, *A Lady's Life in the Rocky Mountains*. p. 55.

19 Henry Nash Smith, *Virgin Land: The American West as Symbol and Myth*, New York: Vintage Books, 1957 [c1950], p. 55.

20 Patricia Nelson Limerick, *The Legacy of Conquest: The Unbroken Past of the American West.* p. 311.

21 Charles William Wilson, *Mapping the Frontier; Charles Wilson's Diary of the Survey of the 49th Parallel, 1858–1862, while Secretary of the British Boundary Commission.* p. 121.

22 Lincoln Vanderbilt, *The New and Wonderful Explorations of Professor Lincoln Vanderbilt, The Great American Traveler, in the Territories of Colorado, Arizona, & Utah ... including the Gorgeous Scenery of the Rocky Mountains and the Sierra Nevadas.* p. 27.

23 T. H. White, *The Once and Future King*, New York: G. P. Putnam – Berkley Medallion, 1966, p. 518.

24 On sportsmanship, see: Dorothy Hammond and Alta Jablow, *The Africa that Never Was; Four Centuries of British Writing about Africa*, New York: Twayne Publishers [1970], pp. 189–90.

25 Janet L. Giltrow, North American Travel Writing. PhD diss., Simon Fraser University, 1980 [1979], pp. 6–7.

26 Charles Wentworth Dilke, *Greater Britain: A Record of Travel in English-Speaking Countries during 1866 and 1867.* p. 121.

27 Donald Worster notes in his essay entitled "The Nature We Have Lost": "One thing is clear to the historian: out of our resulting intellectual confusion we are growing toward a more realistic sense of what the natural world will allow us to do." Donald Worster, *The Wealth of Nature*, New York: Oxford University Press, 1993, p. 13.

28 For more on what he calls "Lords of Yesterday," see: Charles F. Wilkinson, *Crossing the Next Meridian: Land, Water, and the Future of the West*, Washington, DC: Island Press, 1992.

29 George Alfred Lawrence, *Silverland.* p. 247.

30 Paul Fountain, *The Eleven Eaglets of the West*, New York: E.P. Dutton, 1906, p. x.

Bibliography

Abington, S. J. *The "Great West."* London: Educational Trading Company, 1871.

Aflalo, Frederick George. *The Sports of the World.* London: Cassell & Co., 1903.

Abrahams, Roger D., and John F. Szwed, eds. *After Africa: Extracts from British Travel Accounts and Journals of the Seventeenth, Eighteenth, and Nineteenth Centuries concerning the Slaves, their Manners, and Customs in the British West Indies.* New Haven: Yale University Press, 1983.

Armitage, Susan. "Another Lady's Life in the Rocky Mountains," in *Women and the Journey.* eds. Bonnie Frederick and Susan H. McLeod. Pullman: Washington State University Press, 1993. pp. 25–36.

Athearn, Robert G. *Westward the Briton.* New York: Scribner, 1953.

"Babb, James Elisha," *National Cyclopedia of American Biography.* New York: James T. White & Co., 1937. v. 26, pp. 55–56.

Baillie-Grohman, William Adolph. *Camps in the Rockies. Being a Narrative of Life on the Frontier, and Sport in the Rocky Mountains, with an Account of the Cattle Ranches of the West.* New York: C. Scribner's Sons, 1882. Also London: Sampson Low, Marston, Searle, & Rivington, 1882.

Baillie-Grohman, William Adolph. *Fifteen Years' Sport and Life in the Hunting Grounds of Western America and British Columbia.* London: Horace Cox, 1900.

Batts, John Stuart. *British Manuscript Diaries of the Nineteenth Century, An Annotated Listing*. Totowa, NJ: Rowman and Littlefield, 1976.

Bell, Ian. *Dreams of Exile: Robert Louis Stevenson, A Biography*. New York: H. Holt, 1993.

Bennett, Norman R., ed. *Stanley's Despatches to the New York Herald, 1871-1872, 1874-1877*. Boston: Boston University Press, 1970.

Berger, Max. *The British Traveller in America, 1836–1860*. New York: Columbia University Press, 1943.

Berry, Lloyd Eason, and Robert O. Crummey, eds. *Rude & Barbarous Kingdom; Russia in the Accounts of Sixteenth-Century English Voyagers*. Madison: University of Wisconsin Press, 1968.

Bierman, John. *Dark Safari: The Life Behind the Legend of Henry Morton Stanley*. New York: Knopf, 1990.

Big Game Hunting and Angling, vol. 3 of *British Sports and Sportsmen*. London: "The Sportsman," 1914.

Bird, Isabella L. *A Lady's Life in the Rocky Mountains*; with an introduction by Daniel J. Boorstin. Norman: University of Oklahoma Press, 1960.

Birrell, Andrew. "Survey Photography in British Columbia, 1858–1900," *BC Studies* 52 (Winter 1981–82): 39–60.

Boddam-Whetham, J. W. *Western Wanderings: A Record of Travel in the Evening Land*. London: Richard Bentley, 1874.

Bodley, John E. C. Diary, 1888. Bodleian Library. MSS.Eng. misc.e.461.

Bredeson, Robert C. "Landscape description in nineteenth-century American travel literature," *American Quarterly* 20 (1968): 86–94.

Burchell, Robert A. *British Travellers Report on the White Conquest of the Trans-Mississippi West 1865–1905*. London: British Library, 1993. (First annual lecture, the David and Mary Eccles Centre for American Studies, July 1993).

Burton, Richard Francis. *The City of the Saints, and Across the Rocky Mountains to California*. New York: Harper & Brothers, 1862.

Butler, William Francis. *Sir William Butler, an Autobiography*. London: Constable and Company, 1911.

Butler, William Francis. *The Great Lone Land: A Narrative of Travel and Adventure in the North-west of America*. 15th and cheaper ed. London: Sampson, Low, Marston & Co. [1872] 1891?

Butler, William Francis. *The Wild Northland, Being the Story of a Winter Journey, with Dogs, across Northern North America*. New York: Allerton Book Co., [1873] 1922.

Chance, David. "Balancing the Fur Trade at Fort Colville," *The Record* 34 (1973): 22–35.

Cole, Douglas, and Maria Tippitt. "Pleasing Diversity and Sublime Desolation: the 18th Century British Perception of the Northwest Coast," *Pacific Northwest Quarterly* 65 (1974): 1–7.

Combe, William. *The First Tour of Dr. Syntax, in Search of the Picturesque; a Poem*. Illustrated with eighty plates by T. Rowlandson. Ninth edition with new plates. London: Nattali & Bond, [1842].

Conley, Cort. *Idaho Loners: Hermits, Solitaries, and Individualists*. Cambridge, ID: Backeddy Books, 1994.

Davis, John F. "Constructing the British View of the Great Plains," in *Images of the Plains: the Role of Human Nature in*

Settlement, eds. Brian W. Blouet and Merlin P. Lawson. Lincoln: University of Nebraska Press, [1975] pp. 181–85.

Desborough, William Henry Grenfell, 1st Baron. Diary, 1884, America and Canada. MSS.D 86/2 Buckinghamshire Record Office, County Hall, Aylesbury, England.

Dilke, Charles Wentworth. *Greater Britain: A Record of Travel in English-Speaking Countries during 1866 and 1867*. London: Macmillan, 1868.

Dobell, Bertram. "Memoir," in Thomson, James, *City of Dreadful Night*. London: Reeves & Turner, 1895. v. 1, pp. ix–xcii.

Dunae, Patrick A. *Gentlemen Emigrants: from the British Public Schools to the Canadian Frontier*. Vancouver, BC: Douglas & McIntyre, 1981.

Dunraven, Windham Thomas Wyndham-Quin. *The Great Divide: Travels in the Upper Yellowstone in the Summer of 1874*. 2d ed. rev. London: Chatto and Windus, 1876. Reprinted: Lincoln: University of Nebraska Press, 1967.

Eckman, James. *The British Traveler in America, 1875–1920*. PhD diss., Georgetown University, 1946.

Ellmann, Richard. *Oscar Wilde*. New York: Alfred A. Knopf, 1988.

Fedden, Henry Romilly. *English Travellers in the Near East*, by Robin Fedden. London, New York: Published for the British Council by Longmans, Green [1958].

Fender, Stephen. *Plotting the Golden West: American Literature and the Rhetoric of the California Trail*. Cambridge: Cambridge University Press, 1981.

Finlayson, Roderick. Biography (1891) http://collections.ic.gc.ca/salish/trad/rodfin.htm.

"Footnotes to history," *Idaho Yesterdays* 8 (Spring 1964): 33–36.

Fountain, Paul. *The Eleven Eaglets of the West: Travels in California, Oregon, Washington, Idaho, Montana, Wyoming, Colorado, New Mexico, Arizona, Utah, and Nevada*. New York: E. P. Dutton, 1906.

Francis, Francis, Jr. (or, the younger). *Saddle and Mocassin*. London: Chapman and Hall, 1887.

Frantz, Ray William. *The English Traveller and the Movement of Ideas, 1660–1732*. Lincoln: University of Nebraska Press [1967].

Frome, Michael. *Battle for the Wilderness*. New York: Praeger, 1974.

Fussell, Paul. *Abroad: British Literary Travelling Between the Wars*. New York: Oxford University Press, 1980.

Gillespie, Greg. "'I was well pleased with our sport among the buffalo': Big-Game Hunters, Travel Writing, and Cultural Imperialism in the British North American West, 1847–72," *Canadian Historical Review* 83:4 (December 2002): 555–84.

Gillmore, Parker. *A Hunter's Adventures in the Great West*. London: Hurst & Blackett, 1871.

Gillmore, Parker. *Prairie and Forest: A Description of the Game of North America*. London: Chapman and Hall, 1874.

Giltrow, Janet L. *North American Travel Writing*. PhD diss., Simon Fraser University, 1980 [1979].

Grant, George Monro. *Ocean to Ocean; Sandford Fleming's Expedition through Canada in 1872 by the Rev. George M. Grant*. [n.p.]: M. G. Hurtig, 1967 [1873].

Guest, Theodora. *A Round Trip in North America, with Illustrations from the Author's Sketches.* London: Edward Stanford, 1895.

Hammond, Dorothy, and Alta Jablow. *The Africa That Never Was; Four Centuries of British Writing about Africa.* New York: Twayne Publishers [1970].

Hayes, A. A. *New Colorado and the Santa Fe Trail.* New York: Harper & Brothers, 1880.

Honour, Hugh. *The European Vision of America: A Special Exhibition to Honor the Bicentennial of the United States.* Cleveland: Cleveland Museum of Art; Kent, Ohio: distributed by Kent State University Press, 1975.

Hubback, Catherine. Letters, Oakland, CA, 1871–1876, to son John and daughter-in-law Mary, Liverpool. Bodleian Library, Oxford. Ms.Eng.lett.e.150.

Hyde, Anne F. "Cultural Filters: The Significance of Perception in the History of the American West," *Western Historical Quarterly* 25:3 (August 1993): 351–74.

Hyde, Anne F. *An American Vision: Far Western Landscape and National Culture, 1820–1920.* New York: New York University Press, 1990.

Jobe, Joseph. *Extended Travels in Romantic America; Being a 19th Century Journey through the most Picturesque Portions of North America, Reconstructed from Accounts by European Visitors.* Lausanne: Edita, 1966.

Johnson, R. Byron. *Very Far West Indeed; A Few Rough Experiences on the North-West Pacific Coast.* 2nd ed. London: Sampson Low, Marston, Low, & Searle, 1872.

Kane, Paul. *Paul Kane's Frontier; Including Wanderings of an Artist among the Indians of North America, by Paul Kane,* edited with a biographical introduction and a *catalogue raisonne* by J. Russell Harper. Austin: Published for the Amon Carter Museum, Fort Worth, and the National Gallery of Canada by the University of Texas Press [1971].

Kane, Paul. *Wanderings of an Artist among the Indians of North America, from Canada to Vancouver's Island and Oregon, through the Hudson's Bay Company's Territory and Back Again.* Toronto: The Radisson Society of Canada, Limited, 1925.

Kipling, Rudyard. *American Notes: Rudyard Kipling's West,* edited and with an introduction by Arrell Morgan Gibson. New ed. Norman: University of Oklahoma Press, 1981.

Kipling, Rudyard. *Kipling's America: Travel Letters, 1889–1895,* edited by D. H. Stewart. Greensboro: ELT Press, 2003.

Lawrence, George Alfred. *Silverland.* London: Chapman & Hall, 1873.

Legard, Allayne Beaumont. *Colorado.* London: Chapman and Hall, 1872.

Leslie, Shane. *American Wonderland; Memories of Four Tours in the United States of America (1911–1935).* London: M. Joseph, Ltd. [1936].

Leslie, Shane. *Memoir of John Edward Courtenay Bodley.* London: Cape [1930].

Lewis, Lloyd, and Henry Justin Smith. *Oscar Wilde Discovers America, 1882.* New York: B. Blom [1967, c1936].

Limerick, Patricia Nelson. *The Legacy of Conquest: The Unbroken Past of the American West.* New York: Norton, 1987.

Limerick, Patricia Nelson. "The shadows of heaven itself." In *Atlas of the New West: Portrait of a Changing Region*. ed. William Riebsame. New York: W. W. Norton & Company, 1997. pp. 151–78.

Lord, John Keast. *At Home in the Wilderness, by the Wanderer*. London: Robert Hardwicke, 1867.

Lord, John Keast. *The Naturalist in Vancouver Island and British Columbia*. London: R. Bentley, 1866.

Macfarlane, Robert. *Mountains of the Mind*. New York: Pantheon, 2003.

MacLaren, I. S. *The Influence of Eighteenth Century British Landscape Aesthetics on Narrative and Pictorial Responses to the British North American North and West, 1769–1872*. PhD diss., University of Western Ontario, 1983.

Marryat, Francis Samuel. *Mountains and Molehills, or, Recollections of a Burnt Journal, by Frank Marryat; with Illustrations by the Author*. London: Longman, Brown, Green and Longmans, 1855. Reprinted: Time-Life Books. (Classics of the Old West) 1982.

Marshall, Walter Gore. *Through America: or, Nine Months in the United States*. London: Sampson Low, 1881.

Mayne, Richard C. *Four Years in British Columbia and Vancouver Island*. London: J. Murray, 1862.

Mayne, Richard C. "Report on a Journey in British Columbia in the Districts Bordering on the Thompson, Fraser, and Harrison Rivers," *Journal of the Royal Geographic Society* 31 (1861): 213–23.

Merritt, John I. *Baronets and Buffalo: The British Sportsman in the American West, 1833–1881*. Missoula, MT: Mountain Press Pub. Co., 1985.

Mesick, Jane Louise. *The English Traveller in America, 1785–1835*. New York: Columbia University Press, 1922. Reprinted: St. Clair Shores, MI: Scholarly Press, 1970.

Messiter, C. A. *Sport and Adventures among the North American Indians*. London: R. R. Porter, 1890.

Mikes, George. *How to be an Alien*. London: Wingate, 1946.

Mitchell, Lee Clark. *Witnesses to a Vanishing America: the Nineteenth-Century Response*. Princeton: Princeton University Press, 1981.

Monroe, Robert D. "The Earliest Pacific Northwest Indian Photograph (1860)," In *Three Classic American Photographs: Texts and Contexts*, ed. Mick Gidley, *American Arts Pamphlet No. 7*, Exeter: University of Exeter American Arts Documentation Centre, 1982. pp. 12–20.

Morris, Maurice O'Connor. *Rambles in the Rocky Mountains: With a Visit to the Gold Fields of Colorado*. London: Smith, Elder & Co., 1864.

Mouat, Jeremy. "Morley Roberts in the Western Avernus," *Pacific Northwest Quarterly* 93:1 (Winter 2001/2002): 26–36.

Mulvey, Christopher. *Anglo-American Landscapes: A Study of Nineteenth-Century Anglo-American Travel Literature*. Cambridge: Cambridge University Press, 1983.

Murphy, John Mortimer. *Rambles in North-Western America from the Pacific Ocean to the Rocky Mountains, Being a Description of the Physical Geography, Climate, Soil Productions, Industrial and Commercial Resources, Scenery, Population, Educational Institutions, Arboreal Botany and Game Animals of Oregon, Washington territory, Idaho, Montana, Utah and Wyoming*. London: Chapman and Hall, 1879.

Naef, Weston J., and James N. Wood. *Era of Exploration: The Rise of Landscape Photography in the American West, 1860–1885*. Buffalo: Albright-Knox Art Gallery, 1975.

Nash, Roderick. "Qualitative landscape values: the historical perspective," in *Landscape Assessment: Values, Perceptions, and Resources*, ed. Ervin H. Zube, Robert O. Brush, and Julius G. Fabos. Stroudsburg, PA: Dowden, Hutchinson & Ross, 1975.

Nash, Wallis. *Oregon: There and Back in 1877*. London: Macmillan and Co., 1878; reprinted: Corvallis: 1976.

Nash, Wallis. *Two Years in Oregon*. New York: D. Appleton and Company, 1882.

Nevins, Allan. *America through British Eyes*. [New ed. rev. and enl.] New York: Oxford University Press, 1948.

Nicolson, Marjorie Hope. *Mountain Gloom and Mountain Glory; The Development of the Aesthetics of the Infinite*. Ithaca, NY: Cornell University Press [1959].

Nomura, Gail M. "Significant Lives: Asia and Asian Americans in the History of the U.S. West," *Western Historical Quarterly* 25:1 (Spring 1994): 69–88.

North American Boundary Commission Photographs. Royal Engineers Corps Library, Chatham, Kent.

Olson, Jeanne. *Writing the Wild West: Travel Narratives of the late Nineteenth Century Tourist*. PhD diss. Arizona State University, 1996.

Olson, Lee. *Marmalade and Whiskey: British Remittance Men in the West*. Golden: Fulcrum, 1993.

Palmer, H. Spencer. "Report on the Harrison and Lilloet Route, from the Junction of the Fraser and Harrison Rivers to the Junction of the Fraser and Kayosch Rivers, with Notes on the Country beyond, as far as Fountain," *Journal of the Royal Geographic Society* 31 (1861): 224–36.

Paolucci, Henry. *James Thomson's The City of Dreadful Night: A Study of the Cultural Resources of its Author and a Reappraisal of the Poem*. Wilmington: Griffon House for the Bagehot Council, 2000.

Phillips, John C. *A Bibliography of American Sporting Books*. Boston: Edward Morrill and Son, 1930.

Piercy, Frederick Hawkins. *Route from Liverpool to Great Salt Lake Valley*. Edited by Fawn M. Brodie. Cambridge: Belknap Press of Harvard University Press, 1962.

Pomeroy, Earl. *In Search of the Golden West; The Tourist in Western America*. New York: Knopf, 1957.

Price, Rose Lambart. *The Two Americas; An Account of Sport and Travel*. London: Sampson, Low, 1877.

Rae, W. F. *Westward by Rail, The New Route to the East*. London: Longmans, Green & Co., 1870.

Raban, Jonathan. *Passage to Juneau: A Sea and its Meanings*. New York: Pantheon Books, 1999.

Rapson, Richard L. *Britons View America: Travel Commentary, 1860–1935*. Seattle: University of Washington Press, [1971].

Reyburn, Marjorie L. "James Thomson in Central City," *University of Colorado Studies, Series B, Studies in the Humanities* 1:2 (June 1940): 182–203.

Riebsame, William, general ed. *Atlas of the New West: Portrait of a Changing Region*. New York: W. W. Norton & Company, 1997.

Ronnenberg, Herman Wiley. "Cherokee Bob's Grave: The Historical and Literary Legacy from Fabulous Florence," *Echoes of the Past* 1:6 (September 2004): 5–15.

Russell, Charles. *Diary of a Visit to the United States of America in the Year 1883*. New York: United States Catholic Historical Society, 1910.

Rylatt, R. M. *Surveying the Canadian Pacific: Memoir of a Railroad Pioneer*. Salt Lake City: University of Utah Press, 1991.

Salt, Henry Stephens. *The Life of James Thomson ("B. V."), With a Selection from His Letters and a Study of His Writings*. Port Washington, NY: Kennikat Press, 1889 [1972].

Schaefer, William David. *James Thomson, B.V.: Beyond "The City."* Berkeley: University of California Press, 1965.

Schama, Simon. *Landscape and Memory*. New York: Knopf, 1995.

Schreier, Carl. *Field Guide to Yellowstone's Geysers, Hot Springs and Fumaroles*. Moose, WY: Homestead Publishing, 1987.

Schwantes, Carlos A. *Railroad Signatures across the Pacific Northwest*. Seattle: University of Washington Press, 1993.

Seton-Karr, Henry. *My Sporting Holidays*. London: Edward Arnold, 1903.

Seymour-Smith, Martin. *Rudyard Kipling*. New York: St. Martin's Press, 1989 [1990].

Simmons, James C. *Passionate Pilgrims: English Travelers to the World of the Desert Arabs*. New York: W. Morrow, 1987.

Smith, Henry Nash. *Virgin Land: The American West as Symbol and Myth*. New York: Vintage Books, 1957 [c1950].

Snow, Edwina Jo. "British travelers view the Saints, 1847–1877," *Brigham Young University Studies* 31 (1991): 63–81.

South, Colon. *Out West: or, From London to Salt Lake City and Back*. London: Wyman & Sons, 1884.

Southesk, James Carnegie, Earl of. *Saskatchewan and the Rocky Mountains: A Diary and Narrative of Travel, Sport, and Adventure During a Journey Through the Hudson's Bay Company's Territories in 1859 and 1860*. Toronto: J. Campbell, 1875. (Online as part of *Early Canadiana Online*, see http://www.canadiana.org/ECO/ItemRecord/43075?id=b93347c0424ecf8d.)

Spence, Clark C. *British Investments and the American Mining Frontier, 1860–1901*. Ithaca, NY: Published for the American Historical Association, Cornell University Press [1958].

Sprague, Marshall. *A Gallery of Dudes*. Boston: Little, Brown, 1966.

Stanley, Henry M. *The Autobiography of Sir Henry Morton Stanley*, ed. by his wife, Dorothy Stanley. Boston, New York: Houghton Mifflin Company, 1909.

Stanley, Henry M. *My Early Travels and Adventures in America and Asia*. London: Sampson Low, Marston and Company, 1895.

Stevenson, Robert Louis. *From Scotland to Silverado*, ed. James D. Hart. Cambridge: Belknap Press of Harvard University Press, 1966.

Thomson, James. "Religion in the Rocky Mountains" in *The Speedy Extinction of Evil and Misery; Selected Prose of James Thomson (B.V.)*, ed. William David Schaefer. Berkeley: University of California Press, 1967.

Thomson, James. *The City of Dreadful Night; and Other Poems*. Portland, ME.: T. B. Mosher, [n.d.].

Thomson, James. *City of Dreadful Night; Vane's Story; Weddah & Om-El-Bonain; Voice from the Nile; & Poetical Remains*, ed. Bertram Dobell, with a memoir of the author. London: Reeves & Turner, 1895.

Thomson, James. Diary, May 18–Dec 12, 1872. Bodleian Library, Oxford. Ms.Don.e.46.

Thomson, James. Notebook, 1872. Bodleian Library, Oxford. MS.Don.e.47.

Townshend, S. Nugent. *Colorado: its Agriculture, Stockfeeding, Scenery, and Shooting*. London: "The Field" Office, 1879.

Trenton, Patricia, and Peter H. Hassrick. *The Rocky Mountains: A Vision for Artists in the Nineteenth Century*. Norman: University of Oklahoma Press, 1983.

Twain, Mark, and Charles Dudley Warner. *The Gilded Age; A Tale of Today*. Hartford: American Publishing Co., 1873.

Turner, J. Fox. *There and Back or Three Weeks in America*. London: Simpkin, Marshall & Co., 1883.

Turner-Turner, John. "Fur trapping in North America," in *Big Game Hunting and Angling*, vol. 3 of *British Sports and Sportsmen*. London: "The Sportsman," 1914. pp. 123–35.

Turner-Turner, John. "Practical notes," in Frederick George Aflalo. *The Sports of the World*. London: Cassell & Co., 1903. pp. 201–2.

Turner-Turner, John. *Three Years' Hunting and Trapping in America and the Great North-West*. London: Maclure & Co., 1888.

Vanderbilt, Lincoln. *The New and Wonderful Explorations of Professor Lincoln Vanderbilt, the Great American Traveler, in the Territories of Colorado, Arizona, & Utah ... including the Gorgeous Scenery of the Rocky Mountains and the Sierra Nevadas*. London: J. W. Last, 1870.

Venn, George. "Continuity in Northwest Literature," *Marking the Magic Circle*. Corvallis: Oregon State University Press, 1987. pp. 84–109.

Vivian, Arthur Pendarves. *Wanderings in the Western Land. With Illustrations from Original Sketches by Mr. Albert Bierstadt and the Author*. London: Low, Marston, Searle & Rivington, 1879.

Waddington, Alfred P. "On the Geography and Mountain Passes of British Columbia in Connection with an Overland Route," *Journal of the Royal Geographical Society* 38 (1868): 118–28.

Wagner, Tamara S. "Catherine Hubback (1818–1877): An Overview." http://www.victorianweb.org/authors/hubback.

Weeks, Kathleen S. "Monuments mark this boundary," *Canadian Geographical Journal* 31 (September 1945): 120–33.

Wheeler, Douglas L. "Henry M. Stanley's Letters to the Missouri Democrat," *Bulletin of the Missouri Historical Society* (April 1961): 269–86.

White, T. H. *The Once and Future King*. New York: G. P. Putnam – Berkley Medallion, 1966.

Wilde, Oscar, "The American Invasion" (*Court and Society Review*, March 23, 1887) in *Miscellanies*, v. 15, of *The First Collected Edition*. London: Dawsons of Pall Mall, 1969 [1908].

Wilde, Oscar, *The Letters of Oscar Wilde*, ed. Rupert Hart-Davis. New York: Harcourt, Brace & World, 1962.

Wilkinson, Charles F. *Crossing the Next Meridian: Land, Water, and the Future of the West.* Washington, DC: Island Press, 1992.

Williamson, Andrew. *Sport and Photography in the Rocky Mountains.* Edinburgh: David Douglas, 1880.

Wilson, Charles William. *Mapping the Frontier; Charles Wilson's Diary of the Survey of the 49th Parallel, 1858–1862, while Secretary of the British Boundary Commission,* Edited and with an introduction by George F. G. Stanley. Toronto: Macmillan of Canada [1970].

Winther, Oscar Osburn. "The British in Oregon Country: a Triptych View," *Pacific Northwest Quarterly* 58:4 (October 1967): 179–87.

Woods, L. Milton. *British Gentlemen in the Wild West: the Era of the Intensely English Cowboy.* New York: Free Press; London: Collier Macmillan, 1989.

Worster, Donald. *The Wealth of Nature.* New York: Oxford University Press, 1993.

Yagoda, Ben. *The Sound on the Page.* New York: HarperResource, 2004.

Zincke, F. Barham. *Last Winter in the United States, Being Table-Talk Collected during a Tour through the Late Southern Confederation, the Far West, the Rocky Mountains &c.* London: John Murray, 1868.

Index